OpenTelemetry Cookbook

Proven approaches for real-time monitoring and observability on cloud, AI, and modern infrastructures

Zeel Wolf

GitforGits®
ASIAN PUBLISHING HOUSE

Published by: GitforGits

Publisher: Sonal Dhandre

www.gitforgits.com

Printed in India

First Printing: November 2025

ISBN: 978-93-49174-39-9

Cover Design by: Kitten Publishing

Prologue

I'm Zeel Wolf, and I got into OpenTelemetry not for fun or to learn more about it. I came here because I had to.

During my career, I've worked with Linux systems, cloud platforms, distributed applications, and security-sensitive environments. Each system got more complex than the last. There are more services, dependencies spread across networks, and applications aren't just single binaries running on predictable hosts anymore. They became living, breathing, ever-changing systems. But often, the way we saw things didn't match up with the reality on the ground.

At first, the problems were pretty subtle. There was a latency spike that only happened during the busiest times. There was an authentication failure in one service, but it actually originated two hops away. The metrics looked good, but users weren't happy. There were logs, but they were correlated manually and it was a slow process. We didn't find any traces of this, or sometimes there just weren't any traces at all. When incidents occurred, teams spent more time assembling evidence than solving the actual problem. As AI-driven systems became more common, these challenges grew. The models made decisions at speeds that were impossible for humans to keep up with. Pipelines changed a lot over time. And the security boundaries are getting blurrier. When something went wrong, we didn't just ask "what failed?" anymore. We also wanted to know "why did the system behave this way?" The usual monitoring tools didn't have the answers. They showed symptoms, not behavior.

While working on this project, I realized something important about observability. It's not just an optional part of infrastructure, it's actually a foundational engineering element. Even well-designed systems can become opaque under pressure if they don't have consistent signals, standardized context, and reliable pipelines. Even worse, teams often tried to fix this by adding more tools instead of creating a solid telemetry strategy.

For me, OpenTelemetry changed the game. It was the first time I saw a practical path toward unified data observability. This path treats traces, metrics, logs, and context as first-class signals rather than disconnected data sources. Just because OpenTelemetry is open source doesn't mean it's perfect. It didn't make things any simpler. The documentation was all over the place. The examples were usually theoretical. A lot of resources got the concepts across, but they didn't really show how to apply them in the real world. They didn't cover things like Linux systems, Kubernetes clusters, cloud platforms, security controls, and existing applications that couldn't be rewritten from scratch. ***This book was created to address that need.*** I wrote this book for users who don't want to debate observability in abstract terms. It's for those who need to install, configure, instrument, route, filter, visualize, and have alerts ready to go right now. All the recipes in this book are based on real-world experiences. They cover situations where telemetry was missing, unreliable, or incomplete, and where OpenTelemetry provided a workable solution when used correctly. You won't find any long, boring theoretical chapters here. Each recipe builds on the previous ones because observability itself is cumulative. You can't really think about advanced signals until you've got the basics down.

My goal is simple for this book. By the time you finish this book, you should be able to make your systems observable in a way that is intentional, structured, and sustainable. I'm talking about microservices, AI workloads, security monitoring, or hybrid cloud infrastructure.

That's the whole point of this book.

Content

Preface

A hands-on, recipe-driven book that puts OpenTelemetry into immediate use. This cookbook is for IT folks like developers, Linux admins, cloud engineers, backend pros, networking experts, and security practitioners. It's for anyone who wants a proven, hands-on way to keep an eye on, trace, and understand modern systems.

This book gives you step-by-step easy solutions to everyday observability challenges, so you can integrate, configure, and operate OpenTelemetry in dynamic environments. Each chapter focuses on solving problems that are directly relevant to production teams. These problems include installing and bootstrapping the Collector on Linux, wiring telemetry pipelines for traces, metrics, logs, and baggage, and integrating with the platforms that organizations trust for analysis and alerting.

Plus, you'll learn how to:

- Get the OpenTelemetry Collector up and running on Linux, Docker, and Kubernetes.
- Make and adjust pipelines to collect, process, and send out different telemetry signals.
- Use it to develop apps across Python, Go, Java, and Node.js.
- Boost signals with semantic info and resource detectors for more context.
- Integrate with AWS CloudWatch, X-Ray, Elastic, Prometheus, Splunk, Datadog, New Relic, Grafana Tempo, Loki, and Jaeger.
- Make a visual plan for telemetry and set up real-time alerts.

There's no need to get lost in theoretical jargon because OpenTelemetry Cookbook gets right to the meat and potatoes of implementation. Every recipe gives you a clear problem statement, a step-by-step solution, and practical validation. If you're just starting out with observability or want to level up your skills, this book's got you covered with clear steps to understand distributed, cloud-native, and hybrid systems.

You can build a solid foundation for strong, easy-to-spot infrastructure and application settings, one step at a time. This book isn't about offering quick fixes or magic solutions. It gives you a full set of tools and techniques that help professionals improve visibility, performance, and reliability in their own technical landscapes.

GitforGits

Prerequisites

Whether you're a developer, Linux admin, cloud engineer, backend pro, networking expert, or security practitioner, this cookbook has something for you. It's for anyone who wants a tried-and-true, hands-on way to keep an eye, trace, and understand modern systems with OpenTelemetry.

Codes Usage

Are you in need of some helpful code examples to assist you in the programming and documentation? Look no further! Our book offers a wealth of supplemental material, including code examples and exercises.

Not only is this book here to aid you in getting the job done, but you have our permission to use the example code in the programs and documentation. However, please note that if you are reproducing a significant portion of the code, we do require you to contact us for permission.

But don't worry, using several chunks of code from this book in the program or answering a question by citing our book and quoting example code does not require permission. But if you do choose to give credit, an attribution typically includes the title, author, publisher, and ISBN. For example, "OpenTelemetry Cookbook by Zeel Wolf".

If you are unsure whether the intended use of the code examples falls under fair use or the permissions outlined above, please do not hesitate to reach out to us at support@gitforgits.com.

We are happy to assist and clarify any concerns.

Acknowledgement

I owe a tremendous debt of gratitude to GitforGits, for their unflagging enthusiasm and wise counsel throughout the entire process of writing this book. Their knowledge and careful editing helped make sure the piece was useful for people of all reading levels and comprehension skills. In addition, I'd like to thank everyone involved in the publishing process for their efforts in making this book a reality. Their efforts, from copyediting to advertising, made the project what it is today.

Finally, I'd like to express my gratitude to everyone who has shown me unconditional love and encouragement throughout my life. Their support was crucial to the completion of this book. I appreciate the help with this endeavour and the continued interest in my career.

CHAPTER 1: BOOTSTRAPPING OPENTELEMETRY

Overview

This chapter's going to look at all the practical bits of installing and setting up the OpenTelemetry Collector on Linux. I'll show you first how to get the Collector up and running quickly using a package manager, and then we'll take a look at how to deploy it in a containerised environment with Docker, working with custom configuration files and verifying our setup through live logs. If that doesn't work, we'll download and run pre-built Collector binaries, handle permissions, and confirm that our system recognises the binary. We'll also build the Collector from scratch, which gives us total flexibility and control over custom changes. We'll be focusing on automation a lot as we set up the Collector to run as a background Linux service using systemd, making sure it starts with the machine and is managed consistently.

Lastly, we'll set up health check and diagnostics endpoints, which'll give us confidence that our installation works as intended and is ready for production use. This means that by following along, we'll be able to install, validate, and manage the OpenTelemetry Collector on any Linux environment, which will set a firm base for more advanced observability practices that we'll cover in later chapters.

Installing OpenTelemetry Collector

Ideally, a Linux system would be installed with the OpenTelemetry Collector quickly, without having to download source code or use containers. The plan is to use a trusted package manager we've already got on our machine, and then confirm the installation is successful so we can get working on observability pipelines right away.

To do this, we'll use the native package manager to update the system package lists, install the OpenTelemetry Collector, and verify that the binary is in place and functional. This method is quick, reduces errors, and lets us start using OpenTelemetry in minutes.

Update Package Lists

To begin with, we need to update our package lists. For this, simply open the terminal and execute the following:

```
sudo apt-get update
```

This will ensure that our system knows the latest package versions from all configured repositories.

Install OpenTelemetry Collector

With the lists updated, we now then install the OpenTelemetry Collector:

```
sudo apt-get install -y opentelemetry-collector
```

The **-y** flag automatically confirms the installation prompts. It allows the process to complete without interruption.

Verify Collector Binary

Here, we will make sure the collector has installed correctly and is accessible in our terminal. We can check the version with the following command:

```
otelcol --version
```

If the output displays a version string (such as **otelcol version 0.85.0** or similar), the collector is present and ready to use. If the terminal responds with a "command not found" error, we may need to check our installation steps or our system's **PATH** variable.

With this collector in place, we can then certainly move on to setting up configuration folders, assigning permissions, or exploring advanced setup scenarios. If we are ready, we can proceed to the next recipe and expand our OpenTelemetry environment.

Deploying Collector using Docker

We might want to use the OpenTelemetry Collector in a portable and isolated way, especially when dealing with different environments or when we don't want to install new packages directly onto the host. For this, we'll go with Docker, as it gives us the flexibility to run the Collector as a container, keeping our system clean and making it easy to replicate or move our setup. But we sometimes have problems running the Collector in a container, mounting custom configuration files, and confirming the Collector starts up successfully.

As we run the OpenTelemetry Collector as a Docker container, this means we don't have any direct host dependencies and can enjoy the benefits of container isolation. So, we'll get our configuration file from the host into the container, making sure the Collector uses our particular pipeline and exporter settings. We'll also check that the Collector's startup is working by looking at its logs inside the running container, and then we'll move on to the next tasks.

You can follow along with me as I walk through the process on a system where Docker is already installed and running.

Preparing Configuration file

Before running the Collector, we need a configuration file. We can place it anywhere on our host, such as in our home directory or a dedicated folder. For this job, we will create a simple config file called **otel-collector-config.yaml** in our current directory as below:

```yaml
receivers:
  otlp:
    protocols:
      grpc:
      http:
exporters:
  logging:
    loglevel: debug
service:
  pipelines:
    traces:
      receivers: [otlp]
      exporters: [logging]
```

We then save the above script in **otel-collector-config.yaml**.

Running Collector Container

After this, we will then start the OpenTelemetry Collector container, wherein we will mount our configuration file into the container's expected location (**/etc/otelcol/config.yaml**).

We can run the following command:

```
docker run --rm \
  -v "$(pwd)/otel-collector-
config.yaml":/etc/otelcol/config.yaml \
  -p 4317:4317 -p 4318:4318 \
  otel/opentelemetry-collector:latest \
  --config /etc/otelcol/config.yaml
```

In the above script,

- The **--rm** flag cleans up the container after it stops.
- The **-v** flag mounts our config file into the container.
- The **-p** flags map the standard OTLP ports (gRPC 4317 and HTTP 4318) to our host.

- The image name **`otel/opentelemetry-collector:latest`** pulls the latest Collector image.
- The **`--config`** option tells the Collector where to find our config inside the container.

Validating Collector Startup

After running the command, we then keep a watch at the terminal output from the container. We generally look for messages that indicate us that the Collector has started up successfully and is running our configuration. Basically, we want to see lines like:

```
...
Serving Prometheus metrics on :8888/metrics
Everything is ready. Begin running and processing data.
```

Incase, if there are any configuration errors, the Collector logs will display clear error messages. We should fix any issues in our config and restart the container if needed.

Confirming Ports and Accessibility

With the container running, our host now exposes the OTLP endpoints on ports 4317 (gRPC) and 4318 (HTTP). We can test connectivity from another shell or service on our host, or continue with further Collector recipes using these endpoints.

Summary of What We Have Done Together:

- Prepared a minimal Collector configuration file for testing.
- Ran the OpenTelemetry Collector in a Docker container, using a mounted config.
- Validated the startup and checked the logs for successful initialization.
- Exposed the necessary ports for data collection and confirmed we are ready to expand our Collector setup.

We now have the Collector running in an isolated, repeatable Docker environment, ready to be integrated into our observability pipelines. Next, we can add more advanced configuration, or proceed to run the Collector as a Linux service if our use case requires it.

Installing Collector via Pre-built Binaries

There will be challenges wherein we may run into situations like installing OpenTelemetry Collector via package manager or the Docker is not working as expected. Perhaps, it could be that our distribution does not have a supported package, or we want full control over the Collector version without involving containers. So, in such a case, the direct download and then running a pre-built binary is the best way to get the Collector working on our system.

Now here, we can download the official OpenTelemetry Collector binary from the releases page, extract it, assign the correct permissions, and then run it directly. This approach does not depend on system package managers or Docker and gives us flexibility to use any release version we want. After setting up the binary, we can easily run a test using the default configuration bundled with the release, so we know the Collector is working before we move on to customization.

Let us carry out all these steps:

Downloading Latest Collector Release

First, we want to get the URL for the latest release. The OpenTelemetry Collector's official binaries are hosted on GitHub. We will use **wget** or **curl** to download the appropriate tarball for Linux.

For this demonstration, let us choose the latest release version and the right architecture (for most systems, **amd64**).

```
wget https://github.com/open-telemetry/opentelemetry-
collector-releases/releases/latest/download/otelcol-linux-
amd64.tar.gz
```

This downloads the latest Linux Collector tarball to our current directory.

Extracting Tarball

Once the download finishes, we then extract the contents of the tarball, and for this, we use **tar**:

```
tar -xvf otelcol-linux-amd64.tar.gz
```

This creates a directory (often named **otelcol-linux-amd64** or similar) with the binary and default configuration files.

Assigning Execute Permissions

We then move into directory and make sure the binary has correct permissions to execute:

```
cd otelcol-linux-amd64

chmod +x otelcol
```

In the above, the **chmod +x** step confirms that the Collector binary is executable.

Testing Collector Execution

The release archive typically includes a default configuration file (for example, **config.yaml**). We can start the Collector with this configuration to make sure it runs successfully:

```
./otelcol --config config.yaml
```

If everything is set up correctly, we will see the Collector output logs in the terminal, indicating that it has started successfully and is using the default configuration. The output should include startup information and status messages.

This direct installation method ensures we can run the Collector anywhere, independent of package managers or Docker. If we need to customize or upgrade in the future, we only need to repeat the download and extraction steps with a new release.

Building Collector from Source

Sometimes, we may want to use a version of the OpenTelemetry Collector that includes custom patches, experimental features, or is ahead of the standard release cycle. And, the package managers and pre-built binaries do not primarily offer the flexibility or bleeding-edge updates that advanced users require. So, for this reason, building the Collector from source code becomes essential, especially for developers who want to customize components or contribute directly to the project. However, many users find it challenging to build the Collector from upstream sources, due to unfamiliarity with Go, dependency management, or general build processes on Linux.

We can address this problem by walking through each part of the process like, cloning the Collector repository, installing all the required build dependencies, compiling the binary, and finally running our locally built Collector.

In the following we will begin to address the challenge:

Cloning OpenTelemetry Collector Repository

We need the source code of the Collector, which is hosted on GitHub. The official repository name is **open-telemetry/opentelemetry-collector**.

We just have to run the following in the terminal:

```
git clone https://github.com/open-telemetry/opentelemetry-
collector.git
```

This will create a folder named **opentelemetry-collector** in our current working directory. We can move into this directory:

```
cd opentelemetry-collector
```

Now, we have all the upstream code on our machine.

Installing Build Dependencies

The OpenTelemetry Collector is written in Go, so we need the Go toolchain installed. We also need to install the **make** utility, which helps with scripted builds. On most systems, Go can be installed from a package manager, or we can download the official tarball for the latest version.

In case, if we have not installed Go yet, we can check our version with:

```
go version
```

If Go is missing or outdated, we should download and install a version that matches the requirements specified in the repository's **README.md** or **go.mod** file. Go version 1.19 or higher is commonly recommended.

After this, we also confirm that **make** is installed:

```
make --version
```

If **make** is not present, it can be installed with:

```
sudo apt-get install make
```

With this, our system is prepared for the build.

Compiling Collector Binary

For this, inside the **opentelemetry-collector** directory, we use **make** to start the build process. The Collector's repository typically includes a **Makefile** with build targets. So, to build the Collector binary, we use:

```
make otelcol
```

This command downloads the Go dependencies, compile the Collector, and output the binary in the **bin/** directory (usually as **bin/otelcol**).

The build output will display messages about dependency installation and compilation progress. If any errors occur, we should carefully review the terminal output and ensure our Go version and dependencies are correct.

Running Local Collector

After a successful build, our new Collector binary will be located at **bin/otelcol**. We can run this binary with a default or custom configuration file.

To confirm our build is working:

```
./bin/otelcol --version
```

This will display the version string of our custom build.

Next, to start the Collector using a configuration file, we use:

```
./bin/otelcol --config config.yaml
```

If we want to test with the default config, we can create or use a basic configuration file like what we have seen in earlier recipes. The Collector will output logs in the terminal, showing its startup status and confirming that our build is functional.

Running Collector as a Systemd Service

For the OpenTelemetry Collector to run automatically in the background, restart on failure and always be available after a system reboot, it's not reliable to run it as a one-off process or manual command. A lot of teams find it hard to automate the Collector's lifecycle so it starts up with the machine and is managed consistently on Linux servers. We need a way to manage, monitor and control the Collector like any other long-running Linux service.

The Linux system provides a built-in service manager called **systemd** that lets us define custom services, control automatic startup, and manage service status. By creating a systemd service file for the OpenTelemetry Collector, we can easily automate its execution, control it with familiar commands, and guarantee it restarts or stays online as needed. We will create and register a service definition, enable it on boot, and then learn to manage it using **systemctl**.

Creating the Systemd Service File

At first, we will create a service file for OpenTelemetry Collector. The standard location for custom service files is **/etc/systemd/system/**.

```
sudo nano /etc/systemd/system/otelcol.service
```

Now, we then paste the following configuration into the editor:

```
[Unit]
Description=OpenTelemetry Collector
After=network.target
[Service]
Type=simple
```

```
ExecStart=/usr/local/bin/otelcol --config
/etc/otelcol/config.yaml
Restart=on-failure
User=otel
Group=otel
[Install]
WantedBy=multi-user.target
```

In the above example:

- The **ExecStart** points to the Collector binary.
- The **--config** flag should point to the desired Collector configuration file.
- The **User** and **Group** set the privileges. You can use **otel** if you have created a dedicated user, or use **root** for simplicity during testing.

After this, we then just save and exit the editor.

Enabling Boot Start Service

We need to reload the systemd manager configuration to recognize the new service:

```
sudo systemctl daemon-reload
```

Next, we then enable the service to start automatically whenever the system boots:

```
sudo systemctl enable otelcol.service
```

Starting and Managing Collector Service

Next, we then start the service with:

```
sudo systemctl start otelcol.service
```

We can check the status of the service to confirm it is running:

```
sudo systemctl status otelcol.service
```

The output should show the service as "active (running)" with recent log entries from the Collector process.

If we want to stop the service:

```
sudo systemctl stop otelcol.service
```

And, if we want to restart after a configuration change:

```
sudo systemctl restart otelcol.service
```

At any point, if we want to check if the Collector is running automatically:

```
sudo systemctl status otelcol.service
```

If the service shows as active, the automation is working fine and active as desired.

Verifying Collector Health and Diagnostics

After you've installed and got the OpenTelemetry Collector up and running, it's important to have a reliable way to confirm it's all working as expected. If you don't validate things, then things can go wrong without you even noticing. A lot of teams miss issues at this stage because they don't check the built-in health endpoints, ignore the collector logs, or don't confirm that the service is ready before integrating with production applications. We need to find some practical ways to make sure the Collector is healthy and ready for live workloads.

There are built-in health check endpoints and diagnostic extensions in OpenTelemetry Collector that let us check its status directly. If we enable these endpoints in our configuration, we can check them from a browser or terminal to confirm that startup, pipeline readiness and ongoing health are all good. We can also keep an eye on logs for error messages and key events that show things are ready or if there are any problems.

I'll show you how to enable and validate health endpoints and diagnostic extensions, step by step, while checking logs to confirm Collector readiness.

Enabling Health Check and Diagnostics Extension

To begin with, we will first update the Collector configuration to include the **`health_check`** and **`zpages`** extensions. The **`health_check`** extension provides a simple HTTP endpoint for health probing, and **`zpages`** offers in-depth diagnostics for troubleshooting.

Given below is an example of what we can add to our **`config.yaml`**:

```
extensions:
  health_check:
    endpoint: "0.0.0.0:13133"
  zpages:
```

```
    endpoint: "0.0.0.0:55679"
service:
  extensions: [health_check, zpages]
```

In the above configuration:

- The health check endpoint listens on port **13133**.
- The zPages diagnostics endpoint listens on port **55679**.
- Both extensions are activated by listing them under **service.extensions**.

After editing and saving our configuration, we then restart the Collector. If it is managed by systemd, we can simply use:

```
sudo systemctl restart otelcol.service
```

If running manually, we can then stop and start the process again.

Testing Health Endpoint

Now, with the Collector running, we can test the health check endpoint. We can also use **curl** from the terminal:

```
curl http://localhost:13133/health
```

If it is a healthy Collector, it will return:

```
Server is healthy
```

This above response means the service is up, the configuration is valid, and all enabled pipelines have started without errors. Incase, if we get an error or connection refused, then we need to review our config and service logs.

Accessing zPages Diagnostics

The zPages offers real-time diagnostics and pipeline introspection via a web interface. So, for this, within the browser on the Collector host, we will visit:

```
http://localhost:55679/debug/servicez
```

Here, we can view live stats, trace events, and check the state of pipelines. This tool is useful for deep troubleshooting, especially when we want to confirm that traces, metrics, or logs are flowing through the pipelines.

Reviewing Collector Logs

Next, we then review the Collector logs for warnings, errors, or startup confirmations. If running as a systemd service, we simply use:

```
sudo journalctl -u otelcol.service
```

In the output, we need to look for lines indicating the Collector started successfully, any issues with configuration, or pipeline errors. Basically, we want to see messages that confirm all receivers, processors, exporters, and extensions have started, such as:

```
Everything is ready. Begin running and processing data.
```

and

```
Health Check extension is running at: 0.0.0.0:13133
```

If there are any error or warning lines, then they should be addressed before we proceed to integrate with production systems.

Summary

In this chapter, we've gone through all the steps you need to get the OpenTelemetry Collector up and running on a Linux system. We installed the Collector using a system package manager to make things faster and easier, and we also learned how to deploy the Collector in an isolated Docker container. This involved using mounted configuration files and validating successful startup through logs. When the usual installation paths weren't an option, we just downloaded, extracted and ran pre-built binaries, handling permissions and startup verification with precision. We built the Collector from the upstream source, which gave us hands-on experience with cloning the repository, installing the right build dependencies, compiling the Collector, and confirming that our custom build worked.

We also took care of the automation needs by running the Collector as a systemd service, so it could start on boot and be managed like any essential Linux process. To finish off the deployment, we enabled and tested the built-in health check and diagnostics endpoints, making sure the Collector was ready by checking the command line and the logs. At every stage, we worked together, using the terminal, editing configuration files and interpreting output, so that by the end, we were all set to use the Collector as a reliable, maintainable part of our observability infrastructure.

Chapter 2: Building Telemetry Pipelines

Overview

The focus of this chapter is on building practical telemetry pipelines with the OpenTelemetry Collector. First, we'll learn to set up the OTLP receivers that serve as the main endpoints for traces, metrics, and logs from our apps. This will make sure signals can flow into the Collector. Next, we'll integrate the Prometheus receiver to gather system and application metrics, combining cloud-native monitoring and OTel capabilities. Then, we'll set up the file log receiver, which will collect and parse application logs stored on Linux hosts, so nothing important gets missed.

As we move forward, we'll be using key processors like batch, memory limiter, and retry to make our pipelines strong, flexible, and safe when there's a lot of activity. The chapter will also cover enriching signals with custom attributes and metadata, making it easier to organize and analyze observability data. Finally, we'll connect receivers, processors, and exporters to create unified pipelines for all supported signal types, achieving end-to-end data flow within a single configuration.

Configuring OTLP Receivers for Traces, Metrics, and Logs

When we set up the OpenTelemetry Collector as our telemetry gateway, we sometimes struggle to configure endpoints that our applications use to send traces, metrics, and logs. If these OTLP endpoints are not enabled and listening on the correct ports, telemetry from our services never reaches the Collector. Hence, we need to be sure our Collector is properly configured to receive every supported signal, so that our applications and services can start pushing their telemetry data without friction.

To fix it up, we can enable and test OTLP receivers for all major signal types by editing the Collector's configuration file. The OTLP receiver supports traces, metrics, and logs, using both gRPC and HTTP protocols. Once the configuration is in place, we can confirm that the Collector is listening on the right ports, ready to ingest telemetry signals from our instrumented services.

Let us set up the OTLP receivers, editing the Collector's configuration and testing for each signal type in the following:

Editing Collector Configuration file

We open the Collector's configuration file, **`config.yaml`**. And then, we edit it to include the following OTLP receiver configuration:

```
receivers:
  otlp:
```

```
    protocols:
      grpc:
        endpoint: 0.0.0.0:4317
      http:
        endpoint: 0.0.0.0:4318
service:
  pipelines:
    traces:
      receivers: [otlp]
      processors: []
      exporters: [logging]
    metrics:
      receivers: [otlp]
      processors: []
      exporters: [logging]
    logs:
      receivers: [otlp]
      processors: []
      exporters: [logging]
```

With the above commands,

- The **`otlp`** receiver is now enabled for both gRPC and HTTP protocols.
- The endpoints are set to listen on all network interfaces at ports **`4317`** (gRPC) and **`4318`** (HTTP), which are the standard OTLP ports. And,
- Each pipeline (**`traces`**, **`metrics`**, **`logs`**) is wired to receive data from the **`otlp`** receiver and exports to the Collector's internal logging exporter for verification.

We then save the file and restart the collector.

Testing OTLP Endpoints

After this, we then now test whether the Collector is listening for incoming telemetry on the correct ports. For this, we use:

```
ss -tuln | grep 431
```

From the above, we should see entries for both **0.0.0.0:4317** and **0.0.0.0:4318**.

If we have **otel-cli** or another test client available, we can send test traces or metrics to these endpoints and watch the Collector logs for incoming telemetry. With the logging exporter enabled, the Collector prints all received signals to the terminal or service logs.

Reviewing Collector Logs

Finaly, we will check the logs to confirm the Collector is receiving and processing OTLP signals:

```
sudo journalctl -u otelcol.service
```

In the output, we will look for lines that indicate new traces, metrics, or logs are being processed. This step confirms our configuration works for all three signal types.

By editing the configuration file and restarting the Collector, we enabled OTLP receivers for traces, metrics, and logs, set the endpoints on standard ports, and confirmed the readiness of our Collector to handle telemetry from instrumented applications. This forms the basis for all further pipeline work, ensuring our signals have a clear path from application code to analysis.

Integrating Prometheus Receiver for System Metrics

Many teams rely on Prometheus to scrape and store system and application metrics, especially in cloud-native or Kubernetes environments. However, integrating these Prometheus metrics with the OpenTelemetry Collector often proves challenging. We need to collect Linux node metrics and application-level metrics and route them through the Collector for unified observability. If the Prometheus receiver is not configured properly, we miss out on critical infrastructure insights.

So here, we will add and configure the Prometheus receiver in the Collector configuration, specify what targets to scrape (such as local node exporters or application endpoints), and wire those metrics into our Collector pipeline. Once configured, we will validate the setup by checking for received metrics in the logs or via test exporters.

In the following, we can build and verify this integration step by step:

Adding Prometheus Receiver to Configuration

We open our **config.yaml** file and add the Prometheus receiver under the **receivers** section. We will configure it to scrape metrics from a standard local Prometheus exporter, such as the Linux node exporter (commonly available on port **9100**). We can also add any application endpoints that expose Prometheus metrics.

```
receivers:
  prometheus:
    config:
      scrape_configs:
        - job_name: 'linux_node'
          static_configs:
            - targets: ['localhost:9100']
        - job_name: 'demo_app'
          static_configs:
            - targets: ['localhost:8080']
```

In the above configuration:

- The first job scrapes metrics from a Linux node exporter at **`localhost:9100`**.
- The second job targets a sample application exposing Prometheus metrics at **`localhost:8080`**.
- We can add more targets or jobs as our environment requires.

Wiring Prometheus Receiver into Pipeline

Next, we then update the **`service`** section of the config so that Prometheus metrics are received and processed. If we already have pipelines for metrics, we just add the **`prometheus`** receiver. Otherwise, we need to create a new pipeline:

```
service:
  pipelines:
    metrics:
      receivers: [prometheus]
      processors: []
      exporters: [logging]
```

This setup ensures that metrics scraped by the Prometheus receiver are processed and exported to the logging exporter.

After saving the configuration, we then just have to restart the Collector to pick up the changes.

```
sudo systemctl restart otelcol.service
```

Validating Scraping with Test Metrics

To test, we need one or more Prometheus exporters running. For system metrics, the Linux node exporter is a popular choice. If it is not already running, we can start it in a separate terminal:

```
./node_exporter
```

The exporter listens on **:9100** by default and exposes system metrics in Prometheus format.

With the node exporter and our sample application (if available) running, we check the Collector logs for metrics being scraped and processed. Since the pipeline uses the logging exporter, each metric received by the Collector will be printed to the logs.

After this, we then check the logs with:

```
sudo journalctl -u otelcol.service
```

In the output, we look for entries showing metric names and values, such as:

```
ResourceMetrics #0
InstrumentationLibraryMetrics #0
metric_name: node_cpu_seconds_total
```

If we see these entries, the Collector is scraping and receiving Prometheus metrics from our exporters.

Adding Filelog Receiver for Application Logs

When applications write logs to files on Linux servers, it becomes important to capture these logs for centralized observability. If logs are not collected and processed, troubleshooting and monitoring quickly become fragmented. Sometimes, configuring the Collector to read and parse application log files feels complex, especially when the log format varies or file paths change with deployments. So here, we need a way to reliably point the Collector to these files, parse the log lines, and confirm ingestion so logs are visible in our observability pipeline.

The OpenTelemetry Collector offers the **filelog** receiver, which can be configured to tail and parse log files on disk. By setting the correct file paths, specifying parsing rules, and wiring the receiver into our log pipeline, we can ensure that application logs flow into the Collector for further processing and exporting.

Let us work step by step to add the **filelog** receiver, set up log parsing, and confirm log ingestion.

Configuring Filelog Receiver in Collector

We start by editing our Collector's **config.yaml** to add a **filelog** receiver. This receiver will watch one or more log files for new lines and ingest them as telemetry signals.

Following is a sample configuration:

```
receivers:
  filelog:
    include: [ /var/log/myapp/*.log ]
    start_at: beginning
    operators:
      - type: regex_parser
        regex: '^(?P<timestamp>\S+) (?P<level>\w+)
(?P<msg>.*)$'
        timestamp:
          parse_from: attributes.timestamp
          layout: '%Y-%m-%dT%H:%M:%S'
```

In the above,

- The **include** points to the log file location.
- The **start_at: beginning** tells the receiver to read logs from the start of the file. And,
- The **operators** section defines how to parse each log line. In this recipe, a regex splits each line into a timestamp, log level, and message.

Wiring Filelog Receiver into Log Pipeline

Next, we then ensure the **filelog** receiver is included in our logs pipeline under the **service** section:

```
service:
  pipelines:
    logs:
      receivers: [filelog]
```

```
    processors: []
    exporters: [logging]
```

The above setup collects parsed logs and exports them to the Collector's logging exporter for easy testing.

Testing Log Ingestion

To test, we then write a few sample lines into one of the log files being watched by the filelog receiver. For example, in the below, we will append a log entry:

```
echo "2024-05-13T10:22:35 INFO Application started
successfully" >> /var/log/myapp/app.log
```

Next, we then check the Collector logs:

```
sudo journalctl -u otelcol.service
```

After this, we then look for entries that show our log line was ingested, parsed, and exported:

```
ResourceLogs #0
InstrumentationLibraryLogs #0
Timestamp: 2024-05-13T10:22:35
Level: INFO
Message: Application started successfully
```

If the log line appears, our ingestion and parsing are working. If there are parsing errors, we adjust the regex pattern in the config and repeat the test until log lines are extracted as desired.

Applying Processors for Load Safety

As our telemetry traffic grows, we often encounter problems with pipeline overload, dropped data, or Collector crashes. These issues usually surface during periods of high load, causing instability and data loss. The team has found it difficult to implement proper controls in the OpenTelemetry Collector to safely handle load spikes, prevent out-of-memory errors, and ensure reliable data delivery under stress.

We can solve this by introducing three essential processors in our Collector pipeline: the batch processor, the memory limiter processor, and the retry processor. These processors work together to buffer signals, cap memory usage, and retry failed exports, delivering smooth and resilient telemetry pipelines even under demanding workloads.

In the following, we will configure and validate these processors in our Collector setup.

Adding Processors to Configuration

At first, we will add the processors under the **processors** section in our config file:

```
processors:
  batch:
    timeout: 5s
    send_batch_size: 1024
  memory_limiter:
    check_interval: 2s
    limit_percentage: 75
    spike_limit_percentage: 15
  retry:
    enabled: true
    initial_interval: 5s
    max_interval: 30s
    max_elapsed_time: 5m
```

In the above script,

- The **batch** processor groups signal together to optimize sending and reduce pressure on exporters.
- The **memory_limiter** processor ensures the Collector never exceeds a set percentage of available memory, dropping data safely if needed to avoid crashes.
- The **retry** processor automatically resends failed data batches to exporters, increasing reliability when destinations are temporarily unavailable.

Inserting Processors into Pipelines

We then add these processors to the desired pipelines in the **service** section. For a metrics pipeline:

```
service:
  pipelines:
```

```
  metrics:
    receivers: [prometheus]
    processors: [memory_limiter, batch, retry]
    exporters: [logging]
```

You can apply the same structure for **traces** and **logs** pipelines. The order matters: place **memory_limiter** first, followed by **batch**, then **retry**.

Testing Load Handling

To test load handling, generate increased traffic or simulate many metrics and traces being sent to the Collector. One way is to use a load generation tool or increase the frequency of application telemetry export.

Monitor Collector memory and log output. The memory limiter should activate if available RAM usage approaches the configured limit, and dropped data warnings will appear in the logs.

We can check for log entries like:

```
MemoryLimiter is dropping data to stay under memory limit
Batch processor sending batch of size 1024
Retrying export after failure
```

These confirm the processors are active and handling load.

Monitoring Collector Stability

We can track system metrics and Collector logs over time. For this, we can make use of commands like:

```
ps aux | grep otelcol
free -m
sudo journalctl -u otelcol.service
```

Here, we have to watch for Collector restarts, crashes, or error spikes. If any processor logs frequent drops or retries, consider adjusting batch size, memory limits, or retry settings based on system capacity and data volume.

Injecting Service Metadata with Attribute and

Resource Processors

In general, the telemetry signals often lose their value when they lack clear context about where they originate. If traces, metrics, or logs do not include details such as service name, environment, region, or deployment identifiers, troubleshooting and analysis become slow and difficult. So here, we must ensure that every signal arriving at the OpenTelemetry Collector is enriched with this metadata, making it easy to filter, group, and correlate across all our systems.

The OpenTelemetry Collector provides attribute and resource processors that let us inject static or dynamic metadata into every signal passing through the pipeline. So, the solution is that, if we configure these processors, we can certainly add custom tags for service, environment, or region, and ensure this information travels with all traces, metrics, and logs. This approach keeps our observability data organized and searchable, even in complex distributed systems.

Let us try to add service metadata using attribute and resource processors in the following:

Adding Attribute and Resource Processors to Configuration

To begin with, under the **`processors`** section, we add an **`attributes`** processor to inject or update specific tags, and a **`resource`** processor to set resource-level attributes.

```
processors:
  attributes/add_metadata:
    actions:
      - key: deployment.environment
        action: insert
        value: production
      - key: service.version
        action: upsert
        value: 1.2.3
  resource/add_service_info:
    attributes:
      - key: service.name
        value: "billing-api"
      - key: service.namespace
        value: "payments"
```

```
      - key: cloud.region
        value: "us-west-2"
```

The processor names such as **add_metadata** and **add_service_info** can be anything descriptive.

Inserting Processors into Pipelines

Next, we then attach these processors to our pipelines in the **service** section:

```
service:
  pipelines:
    traces:
      receivers: [otlp]
      processors: [resource/add_service_info,
attributes/add_metadata]
      exporters: [logging]
    metrics:
      receivers: [prometheus]
      processors: [resource/add_service_info,
attributes/add_metadata]
      exporters: [logging]
    logs:
      receivers: [filelog]
      processors: [resource/add_service_info,
attributes/add_metadata]
      exporters: [logging]
```

We can apply the above processors to any or all pipelines as needed. It ensures to place resource processors before attribute processors for consistent enrichment.

Testing Metadata Injection

Finally, we now send test telemetry signals to the Collector. Because the logging exporter is enabled, enriched signals appear in the Collector logs. So here, we will look for entries showing our new attributes:

```
service.name: billing-api
service.namespace: payments
deployment.environment: production
service.version: 1.2.3
cloud.region: us-west-2
```

If these attributes are present, the processors are injecting metadata as intended. If anything is missing, we check processor order or config typos and retest. This whole setup dramatically improves the value and usability of our observability data across all downstream analysis and visualization tools.

Creating Multi-Signal Pipelines

A single pipeline for only one signal type may work for basic setups, but in modern observability, we need to collect and process traces, metrics, and logs together. If we wire only one type, we risk incomplete visibility and fragmented monitoring.

So here, we can design a unified Collector configuration that processes traces, metrics, and logs together by explicitly wiring receivers, processors, and exporters for each signal type. In the following, we will build a complete, multi-signal pipeline by connecting everything together in the Collector configuration.

Configuring Receivers

At first, we start with specifying all required receivers under the **`receivers`** section in our **`config.yaml`**. So here, we will use **`otlp`** for application data, **`prometheus`** for metrics, and **`filelog`** for logs in the following:

```
receivers:
  otlp:
    protocols:
      grpc:
        endpoint: 0.0.0.0:4317
      http:
        endpoint: 0.0.0.0:4318
  prometheus:
```

```
    config:
      scrape_configs:
        - job_name: 'node'
          static_configs:
            - targets: ['localhost:9100']
  filelog:
    include: [ /var/log/myapp/*.log ]
    start_at: beginning
    operators:
      - type: regex_parser
        regex: '^(?P<timestamp>\S+) (?P<level>\w+)
(?P<msg>.*)$'
        timestamp:
          parse_from: attributes.timestamp
          layout: '%Y-%m-%dT%H:%M:%S'
```

This thing prepares our Collector to ingest signals from application code, system metrics exporters, and log files.

Setting up Processors

Next, we then define and reuse the necessary processors for enrichment and stability:

```
processors:
  batch:
    timeout: 5s
    send_batch_size: 512
  memory_limiter:
    check_interval: 2s
    limit_percentage: 75
    spike_limit_percentage: 15
  retry:
    enabled: true
```

```
    initial_interval: 5s
    max_interval: 30s
    max_elapsed_time: 5m
  resource/add_service_info:
    attributes:
      - key: service.name
        value: "orders-api"
      - key: environment
        value: "production"
```

The processors are created once and then referenced in the relevant pipelines for each signal type.

Wiring Exporters

For immediate testing, we can make use of the **`logging`** exporter so we can watch output directly in logs. Later, we can swap in exporters for Prometheus, Jaeger, or any backend:

```
exporters:
  logging:
    loglevel: debug
```

Defining Multi-Signal Pipelines

Next, we then link the receivers, processors, and exporters in the **`service.pipelines`** section for each signal:

```
service:
  pipelines:
    traces:
      receivers: [otlp]
      processors: [resource/add_service_info, batch,
memory_limiter, retry]
      exporters: [logging]
    metrics:
      receivers: [otlp, prometheus]
```

```
      processors: [resource/add_service_info, batch, memory_limiter, retry]
      exporters: [logging]
    logs:
      receivers: [otlp, filelog]
      processors: [resource/add_service_info, batch, memory_limiter, retry]
      exporters: [logging]
```

This design confirms to us that every type of telemetry i.e. traces, metrics, or the logs can be ingested, enriched, batched, and exported as a unified workflow.

After saving the configuration, we just restart the Collector to activate the unified pipelines. This whole thing enables reliable, end-to-end observability across all signals. It simplifies the correlation and troubleshooting throughout the stack.

Summary

To sum it up, we figured out how to set up pipelines for traces, metrics, and logs using the OpenTelemetry Collector. We started by getting the OTLP receivers configured to create endpoints for each signal type. We added the Prometheus receiver, which lets us collect Linux system and application metrics through Prometheus exporters. The file log receiver was set up to read and parse application logs from local files, bringing log data into our centralized pipeline. We've got batch, memory limiter, and retry processors to handle changing loads and keep the Collector stable. We've also adjusted their settings and watched how the Collector reacted during simulated loads. We enriched every signal with valuable service, environment, and deployment metadata using attribute and resource processors, ensuring observability data could be filtered and correlated easily.

We finally got traces, metrics, and logs on the same unified pipelines. We did this by linking receivers, processors, and exporters, and we ended up with a single Collector configuration that supports complete telemetry flows. At each step, we checked our work by reviewing logs and output, making sure every piece of data made it through the pipeline as planned. By the time you're done with this chapter, you'll have a flexible, multi-signal telemetry foundation ready for advanced observability.

Chapter 3: Instrumenting Applications with OpenTelemetry SDKs

Overview

In this chapter, we're going to focus on the essential task of adding OpenTelemetry SDKs to our applications so they're ready to send telemetry signals for traces, metrics, and logs. First, we'll install the necessary SDKs and libraries for Python, Go, and Node.js. That way, we can make sure our codebases are ready for observability from the start. Then, we'll move on to configuring OTLP exporters in code, setting endpoint addresses, and checking that signals are flowing into the Collector. Since distributed context is key for meaningful traces, our plan is to enable and test context propagators. That will let us preserve trace IDs and baggage across service and process boundaries.

The chapter's also going to teach us how to boost reliability by tweaking the timeout and retry settings in our exporters. This'll make sure telemetry delivery keeps flowing smoothly, even during temporary outages or network interruptions. By the time you're done with this chapter, you'll have the confidence to instrument any Python, Go, or Node.js application for OpenTelemetry. That means you'll be able to deliver signals reliably, keep traces continuous, and send custom metadata with every request in the distributed systems.

Installing SDKs and Libraries in Applications

Instrumenting applications with OpenTelemetry requires us to introduce language-specific SDKs so that our code can emit traces, metrics, and logs to the Collector. The teams sometimes find it confusing to select and install the right SDK package, especially when working across multiple languages or with existing projects that have never used OpenTelemetry before. So here, the challenge is to add the correct libraries for Python, Go, or Node.js, and to ensure that each environment is ready for further instrumentation and telemetry export.

We can address this by learning to add OpenTelemetry SDKs to codebases in each language. Let us install OpenTelemetry SDKs for all the three most widely used languages in the following:

Installing OpenTelemetry SDK for Python

We start in the root directory of our Python project:

```
pip install opentelemetry-api opentelemetry-sdk
```

If we plan to export traces and metrics, we can also install relevant exporter packages. For example, to send telemetry via OTLP:

```
pip install opentelemetry-exporter-otlp
```

With this, our Python project is ready to emit and export telemetry data.

Installing OpenTelemetry SDK for Go

For Go projects, the OpenTelemetry libraries are managed as Go modules. In the root of our Go module, we execute the following:

```
go get go.opentelemetry.io/otel/sdk@latest
```

If we want to include the OTLP exporter for direct export, we can also add:

```
go get
go.opentelemetry.io/otel/exporters/otlp/otlptrace@latest
go get
go.opentelemetry.io/otel/exporters/otlp/otlpmetric@latest
```

These commands download and add the SDK and exporter packages to our **`go.mod`** file. It makes them ready to import in our application.

Installing OpenTelemetry SDK for Node.js

For Node.js, we simply add the SDK and core libraries to our project using npm:

```
npm install @opentelemetry/api @opentelemetry/sdk-node
```

To enable exporting to OTLP, we add the OTLP exporter:

```
npm install @opentelemetry/exporter-trace-otlp-http
npm install @opentelemetry/exporter-metrics-otlp-http
```

After installing, the Node.js project can initialize telemetry instrumentation and export data to the Collector.

With this, we have prepared Python, Go, and Node.js projects for OpenTelemetry instrumentation by adding the official SDKs and exporter libraries. This whole easy setup enables us to start capturing and emitting traces, metrics, and logs, forming the foundation for deeper instrumentation and observability in our codebase.

Configuring OTLP Exporters

After installing OpenTelemetry SDKs, we need to send our application's telemetry to the OpenTelemetry Collector for centralized processing. If the exporter is not properly configured with the right OTLP endpoint, our traces, metrics, or logs may never reach the Collector. The process of setting up OTLP exporters in code varies between languages, and misconfiguration leads to silent data loss or connection errors.

So here, our goal is to configure and verify OTLP exporters in Python, Go, and Node.js projects, using the correct endpoint addresses, so our telemetry is reliably delivered.

Configuring OTLP Exporter in Python

We add the following code to our Python application:

```
from opentelemetry import trace
from opentelemetry.sdk.resources import Resource
from opentelemetry.sdk.trace import TracerProvider
from opentelemetry.sdk.trace.export import BatchSpanProcessor
from opentelemetry.exporter.otlp.proto.grpc.trace_exporter
import OTLPSpanExporter
trace.set_tracer_provider(
    TracerProvider(
        resource=Resource.create({"service.name": "sample-
python-service"})
    )
)
otlp_exporter = OTLPSpanExporter(
    endpoint="localhost:4317",  # Collector OTLP gRPC endpoint
    insecure=True               # Use insecure if no TLS
)
span_processor = BatchSpanProcessor(otlp_exporter)
trace.get_tracer_provider().add_span_processor(span_processor)
tracer = trace.get_tracer(__name__)
# Emit a test span
with tracer.start_as_current_span("test-span"):
    print("Test span emitted")
```

This script configures the exporter to send spans to the Collector's gRPC OTLP endpoint at **`localhost:4317`**. The test span should appear in the Collector's logs when the application runs.

Configuring OTLP Exporter in Go

In our Go application, we add:

```
import (
    "context"
    "go.opentelemetry.io/otel"

"go.opentelemetry.io/otel/exporters/otlp/otlptrace/otlptracegr
pc"
    "go.opentelemetry.io/otel/sdk/resource"
    sdktrace "go.opentelemetry.io/otel/sdk/trace"
    "go.opentelemetry.io/otel/attribute"
    "time"
)
func main() {
    ctx := context.Background()
    exporter, err := otlptracegrpc.New(ctx,
otlptracegrpc.WithEndpoint("localhost:4317"),
otlptracegrpc.WithInsecure())
    if err != nil {
        panic(err)
    }
    res, _ := resource.Merge(
        resource.Default(),
        resource.NewWithAttributes(
            attribute.String("service.name", "sample-go-
service"),
        ),
    )
    tp := sdktrace.NewTracerProvider(
        sdktrace.WithBatcher(exporter),
```

```go
        sdktrace.WithResource(res),
    )
    otel.SetTracerProvider(tp)
    tracer := otel.Tracer("example.com/trace")
    _, span := tracer.Start(ctx, "test-span")
    time.Sleep(100 * time.Millisecond)
    span.End()
}
```

Running this program sends a span named "test-span" to the Collector at **localhost:4317**.

Configuring OTLP Exporter in Node.js

Here, we configure the OTLP exporter as shown below:

```javascript
const { NodeTracerProvider } = require('@opentelemetry/sdk-trace-node');
const { OTLPTraceExporter } = require('@opentelemetry/exporter-trace-otlp-http');
const { SimpleSpanProcessor } = require('@opentelemetry/sdk-trace-base');
const { trace, context } = require('@opentelemetry/api');
const provider = new NodeTracerProvider();
const exporter = new OTLPTraceExporter({
  url: 'http://localhost:4318/v1/traces', // OTLP HTTP endpoint
});
provider.addSpanProcessor(new SimpleSpanProcessor(exporter));
provider.register();
const tracer = trace.getTracer('sample-node-service');
const span = tracer.startSpan('test-span');
span.end();
console.log('Test span emitted');
```

This configuration sends trace data to the Collector's HTTP OTLP endpoint at **localhost:4318/v1/traces**.

After running each example, we can check the Collector logs to verify the test span was received. The test runs confirm that our exporter configuration and establish a working link between the application and the Collector. It allows us to proceed with deeper instrumentation.

Using Propagators for Context and Baggage

When services communicate in a distributed system, we need to ensure that traces, context, and any custom metadata (baggage) flow seamlessly between all components. Without proper context propagation, each service sees only its local activity, making end-to-end tracing and troubleshooting almost impossible. So here, our challenge is to enable context propagation so traces remain continuous, and to carry baggage across process and service boundaries for complete observability.

In the following, we will enable and configure context propagation in our application code, using OpenTelemetry's built-in propagators. By setting up and testing propagators, we can ensure that each new span retains the parent context, and that any custom baggage (such as user IDs, tenant tags, or request IDs) travels with the trace across network hops.

In the below, we will work through the setup and validation in Python, Go, and Node.js projects.

Enabling Propagators in Python

We will use the W3C Trace Context and Baggage propagators, which are the OpenTelemetry defaults.

```
from opentelemetry import trace, propagate, baggage
from opentelemetry.sdk.trace import TracerProvider
from opentelemetry.sdk.trace.export import BatchSpanProcessor
from opentelemetry.exporter.otlp.proto.grpc.trace_exporter
import OTLPSpanExporter
trace.set_tracer_provider(TracerProvider())
tracer = trace.get_tracer(__name__)
# Inject baggage
context = baggage.set_baggage("user_id", "alice")
# Propagate context with span
```

```
with tracer.start_as_current_span("parent-span",
context=context) as parent_span:
    print("Trace ID:",
parent_span.get_span_context().trace_id)
    print("Baggage user_id:", baggage.get_baggage("user_id",
context))
    # Simulate outbound request: inject context into headers
    headers = {}
    propagate.inject(headers, context=context)
    print("Injected headers:", headers)
    # Simulate incoming request: extract context from headers
    new_context = propagate.extract(headers)
    with tracer.start_as_current_span("child-span",
context=new_context) as child_span:
        print("Child Trace ID:",
child_span.get_span_context().trace_id)
        print("Baggage in child:",
baggage.get_baggage("user_id", new_context))
```

When running this script, we confirm the child span shares the same trace ID and that baggage is preserved and accessible.

Enabling Propagators in Go

The Go SDK uses the global propagator registry, typically set to the W3C Trace Context and Baggage.

```
import (
    "context"
    "fmt"
    "go.opentelemetry.io/otel"
    "go.opentelemetry.io/otel/attribute"
    "go.opentelemetry.io/otel/baggage"
    "go.opentelemetry.io/otel/propagation"
```

```
    "go.opentelemetry.io/otel/trace"
    "go.opentelemetry.io/otel/sdk/trace"

"go.opentelemetry.io/otel/exporters/otlp/otlptrace/otlptracegr
pc"
    "go.opentelemetry.io/otel/sdk/resource"
    sdktrace "go.opentelemetry.io/otel/sdk/trace"
    "time"
    "net/http"
)
func main() {
    otel.SetTextMapPropagator(
        propagation.NewCompositeTextMapPropagator(
            propagation.TraceContext{}, propagation.Baggage{},
        ),
    )
    ctx := baggage.ContextWithValues(context.Background(),
attribute.String("user_id", "alice"))
    tracer := otel.Tracer("example.com/trace")
    ctx, parentSpan := tracer.Start(ctx, "parent-span")
    fmt.Println("Trace ID:",
parentSpan.SpanContext().TraceID())
    fmt.Println("Baggage user_id:", baggage.Value(ctx,
"user_id"))
    // Inject context to outgoing HTTP headers
    headers := http.Header{}
    otel.GetTextMapPropagator().Inject(ctx,
propagation.HeaderCarrier(headers))
    fmt.Println("Injected headers:", headers)
    // Extract context from headers in a receiving service
```

```
    extractedCtx :=
otel.GetTextMapPropagator().Extract(context.Background(),
propagation.HeaderCarrier(headers))

    _, childSpan := tracer.Start(extractedCtx, "child-span")

    fmt.Println("Child Trace ID:",
childSpan.SpanContext().TraceID())

    fmt.Println("Baggage in child:",
baggage.Value(extractedCtx, "user_id"))

    childSpan.End()

    parentSpan.End()

}
```

This sample demonstrates end-to-end propagation, showing trace continuity and baggage presence.

Enabling Propagators in Node.js

The Node.js uses propagators and baggage via the OpenTelemetry API:

```
const { NodeTracerProvider } = require('@opentelemetry/sdk-
trace-node');

const { W3CTraceContextPropagator, W3CBaggagePropagator } =
require('@opentelemetry/core');

const { context, trace, propagation, baggage } =
require('@opentelemetry/api');

const provider = new NodeTracerProvider();

provider.register({

  propagator: propagation.createCompositePropagator([

    new W3CTraceContextPropagator(),

    new W3CBaggagePropagator(),

  ]),

});

const tracer = trace.getTracer('sample-node-service');

let ctx = baggage.setBaggage(context.active(), { user_id: {
value: "alice" } });
```

```
const parentSpan = tracer.startSpan('parent-span', undefined,
ctx);
console.log("Trace ID:", parentSpan.spanContext().traceId);
const carrier = {};
propagation.inject(trace.setSpan(ctx, parentSpan), carrier);
console.log("Injected headers:", carrier);
const extractedContext = propagation.extract(context.active(),
carrier);
const childSpan = tracer.startSpan('child-span', undefined,
extractedContext);
console.log("Child Trace ID:",
childSpan.spanContext().traceId);
const extractedBaggage = baggage.getBaggage(extractedContext);
console.log("Baggage in child:",
extractedBaggage.getEntry("user_id").value);
childSpan.end();
parentSpan.end();
```

This code confirms that context and baggage flow through propagation, and both trace ID and custom metadata remain intact.

By configuring propagators and testing with real traces and baggage, we preserve distributed context across every process and service. It makes the end-to-end observability truly possible.

Setting SDK Timeouts and Retries

In distributed systems, network interruptions, slow connections, or backend downtime generally cause the telemetry export attempts to fail. If SDKs do not have properly configured timeouts and retries, our traces and metrics may be lost, leading to incomplete observability and gaps in monitoring.

So here, the solution is, that we can explicitly set timeout and retry parameters in the SDK exporter configuration for Python, Go, and Node.js. This will help us to control how long the SDK waits for a response and how many times it tries to resend failed data.

Let us walk through the process in the following:

Configuring Timeouts and Retries in Python

The Python OTLP exporter provides options for timeout and retry through its constructor and environment variables.

Following is the sample script:

```
from opentelemetry.exporter.otlp.proto.grpc.trace_exporter
import OTLPSpanExporter

from opentelemetry.sdk.trace.export import BatchSpanProcessor

from opentelemetry.sdk.trace import TracerProvider

from opentelemetry import trace

trace.set_tracer_provider(TracerProvider())

exporter = OTLPSpanExporter(

    endpoint="localhost:4317",

    timeout=5  # Timeout in seconds for a request

)

span_processor = BatchSpanProcessor(exporter,
schedule_delay_millis=5000)

trace.get_tracer_provider().add_span_processor(span_processor)

# The SDK retries failed exports by default. To adjust retry
behavior,

# set OTEL_EXPORTER_OTLP_RETRY_ENABLED and related variables
in the environment.
```

Set environment variables for advanced retry behavior:

```
export OTEL_EXPORTER_OTLP_RETRY_ENABLED=true

export OTEL_EXPORTER_OTLP_RETRY_MAX_ATTEMPTS=5
```

Configuring Timeouts and Retries in Go

The Go's OTLP exporter lets us control timeout and retry via exporter and BatchSpanProcessor options.

Given below is a quick sample script:

```
import (

    "context"
```

```
    "time"

"go.opentelemetry.io/otel/exporters/otlp/otlptrace/otlptracegr
pc"
    "google.golang.org/grpc"
)
ctx := context.Background()
exporter, err := otlptracegrpc.New(ctx,
    otlptracegrpc.WithEndpoint("localhost:4317"),
    otlptracegrpc.WithInsecure(),
    otlptracegrpc.WithTimeout(5*time.Second), // Request
timeout
    otlptracegrpc.WithDialOption(grpc.WithBlock()),
)
if err != nil {
    panic(err)
}
// BatchSpanProcessor will handle retry logic internally.
// To fine-tune retries, use the WithMaxExportBatchSize and
WithMaxQueueSize options.
```

Configuring Timeouts and Retries in Node.js

The Node.js OTLP HTTP exporter accepts timeout as an option. Retrying failed requests can be handled at the process level or with a custom wrapper, as the core SDK does not automatically retry failed requests.

Following is a snapshot of the script:

```
const { OTLPTraceExporter } =
require('@opentelemetry/exporter-trace-otlp-http');
const { BatchSpanProcessor } = require('@opentelemetry/sdk-
trace-base');
const exporter = new OTLPTraceExporter({
```

```
  url: 'http://localhost:4318/v1/traces',
  timeoutMillis: 5000 // 5 seconds timeout
});
const { NodeTracerProvider } = require('@opentelemetry/sdk-trace-node');
const provider = new NodeTracerProvider();
provider.addSpanProcessor(new BatchSpanProcessor(exporter));
provider.register();
```

For retries, we can wrap exporter logic or use a network library that includes retry features, or rely on a batch processor to handle queued spans until export succeeds.

Simulating Outages and Observing Fallback

With timeout and retry configured, we can simulate a Collector outage by stopping or blocking the Collector process or network port.

```
sudo systemctl stop otelcol.service
```

Or, we can do it by using a firewall rule to block the Collector port.

Now, when the application tries to export spans or metrics, the exporter waits for the configured timeout and then attempts retries. The logs or the terminal output will show retry attempts, warnings, or dropped telemetry.

So here, we restore the Collector:

```
sudo systemctl start otelcol.service
```

Once the Collector is available again, the SDK will resume successful exports. We review logs or application output to confirm that the exporter behaved according to the settings, buffering data if possible and retrying within the configured limits.

Summary

To sum it up, we figured out how to incorporate application telemetry into our OpenTelemetry Collector pipelines using the official SDKs for Python, Go, and Node.js. We started by installing the right language-specific libraries, making sure each codebase could emit traces, metrics, and logs. After we got everything set up, we configured the OTLP exporters in our application code, pointed them to the Collector's endpoint, and checked that we could connect by emitting test spans or metrics. We focused on preserving context and baggage as telemetry traveled through distributed services, enabling propagators and confirming that trace IDs and custom baggage remained continuous across requests. We also tuned the timeout and retry settings in each SDK, so that if there's a transient network issue or a Collector outage, you won't lose telemetry.

We did some simulations to see how each SDK would respond, and we checked the logs and the exporter status to make sure the data was buffered or retried according to our configuration. During the process, every code snippet and setting was shown step-by-step, so by the end of the chapter, we had set up a reliable flow from application code to the OpenTelemetry Collector, with all signals preserved and reliably delivered even under imperfect network conditions.

CHAPTER 4: CODE-BASED INSTRUMENTATION AND AUTO-INSTRUMENTATION

Overview

This chapter's going to teach you how to make apps more observable using both automatic and manual methods across popular programming languages. We'll start with Python and see how to turn on tracing and metrics for web and CLI projects using the OpenTelemetry auto-instrumentation CLI, and all without changing any application code. Next, we'll check out how to add tracing to Java applications by attaching the OpenTelemetry agent at startup, instantly generating telemetry for supported frameworks.

Next, we'll move on to Go, where we'll get hands-on experience with manual tracing by importing the SDK, creating spans in business functions, and propagating context across goroutines and handlers for full trace continuity. To wrap things up, we'll define and measure custom application metrics using the SDK APIs in Python, Go, and Node.js. This'll let us track business KPIs and other key signals specific to our services. All the recipes will give us hands-on, step-by-step instructions to help us create valuable data in a bunch of different situations, making it simpler to keep an eye on, study, and improve distributed systems.

Auto-Instrumenting Python Applications

In many situations, adding manual instrumentation to every function, class, or HTTP handler in a Python application is not practical, especially when time or code complexity is a concern. Teams need a quick, low-effort method to generate traces and metrics from Python web services or CLI tools without rewriting large parts of the codebase. The challenge is to enable tracing and metrics across frameworks with as few changes as possible.

The OpenTelemetry provides a Python auto-instrumentation CLI tool that detects popular frameworks and libraries in a project, then injects tracing and metrics at runtime. Using it, we can activate telemetry by launching our application through a simple command-line wrapper, without touching application source code.

In the following, we will run the above steps to set up and test Python auto-instrumentation.

Installing Auto-Instrumentation Tools

We will at first begin with installing the auto-instrumentation package. So, in our project environment, we will run the following:

```
pip install opentelemetry-instrumentation
pip install opentelemetry-exporter-otlp
```

We then add more instrumentation packages for specific frameworks as needed, for example, Flask, Django, Requests, or SQLAlchemy.

And, before instrumenting our app, we need the Collector running with an OTLP receiver listening on **localhost:4317** (gRPC) or **localhost:4318** (HTTP). These we can use as our endpoints for exporting spans and metrics.

Launching Application with Auto-Instrumentation

Fro a moment, we will think differently in this recipe, wherein we will not modify the Python source code. Instead, we will launch our app using OpenTelemetry instrument command, in which we will specify the OTLP exporter and endpoint.

So here, for a typical web or CLI application such as a Flask app, our command will look something like:

```
opentelemetry-instrument \
  --traces_exporter otlp \
  --metrics_exporter otlp \
  --exporter_otlp_endpoint localhost:4317 \
  python app.py
```

Here, we will replace **app.py** with the entry point of our application. The **--traces_exporter** and **--metrics_exporter** enable exporting both signals. And, the **--exporter_otlp_endpoint** points to the Collector.

If we want to use HTTP instead of gRPC, we can specify the HTTP exporter and change the endpoint.

Span Output

With the application running under the instrument wrapper, we interact with our service as usual like to send the HTTP requests, and invoke the CLI commands, etc. So here, the OpenTelemetry instrumentation hooks into supported libraries and automatically creates spans and metrics as requests flow through the app.

And, to validate, we will check the Collector's logging exporter for an output like the following one:

```
ResourceSpans #0
InstrumentationLibrarySpans #0
Span #0
    name: /api/v1/resource
    status:
```

```
    code: UNSET
...
```

We should see spans corresponding to HTTP routes, database queries, external calls, and other instrumented events.

This thing will confirm that the observability is active and effective with very little effort.

Instrumenting Java with OpenTelemetry Agent

A lot of Java applications are used in production environments where making code changes isn't something you want to do, or even if you could do it, it wouldn't be possible. And let's be real, manually adding tracing logic or tweaking source code for telemetry can be slow and risky, especially for legacy or third-party apps. The teams need a practical method to enable tracing in Java applications instantly, with zero code changes, while making sure that spans are generated and exported to the OpenTelemetry Collector for analysis.

There's an OpenTelemetry Java agent that lets you automatically instrument Java applications by attaching the agent at JVM startup. This agent finds and monitors popular Java frameworks, libraries, and containers during runtime, automatically creating traces for HTTP calls, database queries, messaging, and more. If we specify the Collector endpoint as an environment variable or JVM argument, we can export telemetry directly from the agent without touching the application source code.

I'll walk us through adding tracing to a Java application with the OpenTelemetry agent and making sure telemetry is flowing to the Collector.

Downloading OpenTelemetry Java Agent

First, we will download the latest OpenTelemetry Java agent JAR file from the official GitHub releases page:

```
wget https://github.com/open-telemetry/opentelemetry-java-instrumentation/releases/latest/download/opentelemetry-javaagent.jar
```

This above command downloads the agent jar to our working directory.

Setting Collector Endpoint

By default, the agent sends telemetry to **`localhost:4317`** using OTLP over gRPC. If our Collector is running with the OTLP receiver enabled on that port, we can proceed. To specify another endpoint or use OTLP over HTTP, we set the **`OTEL_EXPORTER_OTLP_ENDPOINT`** environment variable as shown below:

```
export OTEL_EXPORTER_OTLP_ENDPOINT=http://localhost:4318
```

We can also set other environment variables for service name and resource attributes:

```
export OTEL_SERVICE_NAME=sample-java-app
export OTEL_RESOURCE_ATTRIBUTES=deployment.environment=staging
```

Starting Java Application with Agent Attached

Now, to instrument the app, we simply add the **`-javaagent`** flag to the JVM startup command, pointing it to the downloaded agent JAR.

If the usual command is:

```
java -jar app.jar
```

We just change it to:

```
java -javaagent:opentelemetry-javaagent.jar -jar app.jar
```

While doing this, no changes to **`app.jar`** or source code are needed. The agent just hooks into supported frameworks and starts emitting traces immediately.

Reviewing Auto-Generated Telemetry

With the app now running, we generate some activity, such as sending HTTP requests to endpoints exposed by the service or triggering background jobs. If w simply just want to validate it, we just check the Collector's logs to see entries like:

```
ResourceSpans #0
InstrumentationLibrarySpans #0
Span #0
    name: /api/orders
    status:
    code: UNSET
    attributes:
        http.method: POST
```

```
        http.status_code: 200
```

The spans should appear for incoming HTTP requests, database queries, external HTTP calls, and other supported operations. The resource attributes also should reflect the values we set via environment variables.

With this above setup, we have successfully enabled tracing without code modification. In addition, the auto-generated telemetry also appears in the Collector, which confirms the agent's effectiveness for rapid, risk-free observability in any sort of Java environment.

Manual Tracing in Go Applications

Sometimes automated instrumentation is not enough for Go applications, especially when custom business logic, complex goroutines, or unique workflows are involved. In these situations, we need to manually create spans to capture detailed timing and relationships within our Go code. Teams want to know how to directly control tracing, measure specific functions or handlers, and propagate context across goroutines and service boundaries for complete, accurate observability.

So, in this recipe, we will manually add tracing to Go code by importing the OpenTelemetry Go SDK, and then initializing a tracer provider, and finally creating spans at key points in our application. And after this, we will then propagate context through function calls and goroutines, ensuring that parent-child relationships are preserved throughout the workflow.

Following are the steps to realize the above plan:

Importing SDK and Initializing Tracer

At first, we make sure our Go module includes the necessary dependencies:

```
go get go.opentelemetry.io/otel/sdk@latest
go get
go.opentelemetry.io/otel/exporters/otlp/otlptrace/otlptracegrp
c@latest
```

Next, in our Go code, we will then import the needed packages:

```
import (
    "context"
    "fmt"
    "time"
    "go.opentelemetry.io/otel"
```

```
    "go.opentelemetry.io/otel/trace"

"go.opentelemetry.io/otel/exporters/otlp/otlptrace/otlptracegr
pc"
    sdktrace "go.opentelemetry.io/otel/sdk/trace"
)
```

After this, we will initialize the tracer provider and OTLP exporter:

```
ctx := context.Background()
exporter, err := otlptracegrpc.New(ctx,
    otlptracegrpc.WithInsecure(),
    otlptracegrpc.WithEndpoint("localhost:4317"),
)
if err != nil {
    panic(err)
}
tp := sdktrace.NewTracerProvider(
    sdktrace.WithBatcher(exporter),
)
otel.SetTracerProvider(tp)
```

Creating Spans Manually

With the tracer provider ready, we can now manually create spans to measure important sections of code.

```
tracer := otel.Tracer("custom-tracing-demo")
func processOrder(ctx context.Context, orderID string) {
    ctx, span := tracer.Start(ctx, "processOrder")
    defer span.End()
    // Simulate work
    time.Sleep(200 * time.Millisecond)
```

```
    span.AddEvent(fmt.Sprintf("Order processed: %s", orderID))
}
```

In this function, a new span named "processOrder" is created, attached to the parent context, and ended after the logic completes

Propagating Context across Goroutines

And when we start new goroutines, we've got to pass the current context so child spans are attached to their parent right.

```
func handler(ctx context.Context) {
    ctx, span := tracer.Start(ctx, "handler")
    defer span.End()
    // Start a child goroutine, passing the context
    go func(ctx context.Context) {
        ctx, span := tracer.Start(ctx, "background-task")
        defer span.End()
        time.Sleep(100 * time.Millisecond)
    }(ctx)
    time.Sleep(300 * time.Millisecond)
}
```

This thing ensures that there is trace continuity between the handler and the background task.

And then, we call these functions in our application entry point:

```
func main() {
    ctx := context.Background()
    handler(ctx)
    processOrder(ctx, "order-123")
    time.Sleep(500 * time.Millisecond) // Allow time for spans
to export
}
```

After running the application, we check the Collector's logs or tracing backend. Here, we should see "handler," "background-task," and "processOrder" spans, all sharing the same trace context.

This whole process allows us to capture detailed application behavior, maintain parent-child relationships, and send rich, actionable traces to the Collector for analysis.

Creating Custom Metrics Using SDKs

The standard metrics, that we get from the system libraries or the auto-instrumentation gives us only a partial picture of application performance. For meaningful observability, we often need to define custom metrics that reflect business KPIs, such as user signups, payment failures, queue depths, or custom cache hits. There is a need to use the OpenTelemetry SDK to define and emit these application-specific metrics, and then observe them through the Collector for real-time analysis and alerting.

So here, the solution is that, we can use the OpenTelemetry SDK in Python, Go, and Node.js to define custom counters and recorders, and then increment them at important business logic points, and finally emit the data to the Collector using the OTLP exporter. And, if we get to review these metrics in the Collector's output, we can easily confirm that our custom KPIs are visible and available for downstream processing or visualization.

In the following, we will learn to create and emit a custom metric in each of the three primary languages, and then we will also verify the results in the Collector.

Emitting Custom Metrics in Python

First, ensure that the required OpenTelemetry metrics packages are installed:

```
pip install opentelemetry-sdk opentelemetry-api opentelemetry-exporter-otlp opentelemetry-sdk-metrics
```

And with the following script, we can create a custom counter:

```
from opentelemetry.sdk.metrics import MeterProvider

from opentelemetry.sdk.metrics.export import PeriodicExportingMetricReader

from opentelemetry.exporter.otlp.proto.grpc.metric_exporter import OTLPMetricExporter

from opentelemetry.metrics import get_meter_provider

exporter = OTLPMetricExporter(endpoint="localhost:4317", insecure=True)
```

```
reader = PeriodicExportingMetricReader(exporter,
export_interval_millis=5000)
provider = MeterProvider(metric_readers=[reader])
get_meter_provider().set_meter_provider(provider)
meter = provider.get_meter("custom-metrics-demo")
order_counter = meter.create_counter("orders_processed",
unit="1", description="Number of processed orders")
order_counter.add(1, {"status": "success"})
order_counter.add(2, {"status": "failed"})
print("Custom metrics emitted.")
```

This script creates a custom counter for processed orders, emits values, and sends them to the Collector's OTLP endpoint.

Emitting Custom Metrics in Go

Like Python, for Go too, we will add the following:

```
import (
    "context"
    "time"
    "go.opentelemetry.io/otel"

"go.opentelemetry.io/otel/exporters/otlp/otlpmetric/otlpmetric
grpc"
    sdkmetric "go.opentelemetry.io/otel/sdk/metric"
    "go.opentelemetry.io/otel/metric"
    "go.opentelemetry.io/otel/attribute"
)
func main() {
    ctx := context.Background()
    exporter, _ := otlpmetricgrpc.New(ctx,
otlpmetricgrpc.WithInsecure(),
otlpmetricgrpc.WithEndpoint("localhost:4317"))
```

```
    provider :=
sdkmetric.NewMeterProvider(sdkmetric.WithReader(sdkmetric.NewP
eriodicReader(exporter)))
    meter := provider.Meter("custom-metrics-demo")
    counter, _ := meter.Int64Counter("orders_processed")
    counter.Add(ctx, 1, attribute.String("status", "success"))
    counter.Add(ctx, 2, attribute.String("status", "failed"))
    time.Sleep(6 * time.Second) // Allow time for export
    println("Custom metrics emitted.")
}
```

This Go example defines and sends a custom metric to the Collector.

Emitting Custom Metrics in Node.js

For Node.js as well, we will install the needed packages for metrics and create custom counter for the metrics:

```
npm install @opentelemetry/sdk-metrics
@opentelemetry/exporter-metrics-otlp-http
const { MeterProvider, PeriodicExportingMetricReader } =
require('@opentelemetry/sdk-metrics');
const { OTLPMetricExporter } =
require('@opentelemetry/exporter-metrics-otlp-http');
const exporter = new OTLPMetricExporter({ url:
'http://localhost:4318/v1/metrics' });
const reader = new PeriodicExportingMetricReader({ exporter,
exportIntervalMillis: 5000 });
const meterProvider = new MeterProvider({ readers: [reader]
});
const meter = meterProvider.getMeter('custom-metrics-demo');
const orderCounter = meter.createCounter('orders_processed', {
description: 'Number of processed orders' });
orderCounter.add(1, { status: 'success' });
orderCounter.add(2, { status: 'failed' });
```

```
console.log("Custom metrics emitted.");
setTimeout(() => process.exit(0), 6000); // Allow time for export
```

Viewing Metrics in Collector

After running the above examples, open the Collector logs or configured exporter backend. When the Collector is using a logging exporter, look for output such as:

```
ResourceMetrics #0
Metric #0
    name: orders_processed
    attributes: status=success, value=1
Metric #1
    name: orders_processed
    attributes: status=failed, value=2
```

These above lines will confirm to us that the custom metrics have been received and are available for further use.

By defining, emitting, and verifying custom application metrics through SDK APIs, we gain visibility into business-specific KPIs, allowing data-driven decision-making and timely operational response.

Summary

Throughout this chapter, we focused on code-based and automatic instrumentation for several key programming environments. We learned to use the OpenTelemetry Python auto-instrumentation CLI to quickly enable tracing and metrics for web and CLI applications with minimal changes, validating our work by observing generated spans in the Collector. We explored Java agent-based instrumentation, attaching the OpenTelemetry agent to JVM startup, and observed how the agent captured telemetry from supported frameworks without requiring code modification. For Go, we practiced manual tracing by importing the OpenTelemetry SDK, initializing tracers, creating custom spans around specific business logic and goroutines, and propagating context to maintain accurate parent-child span relationships.

Finally, we defined and emitted custom metrics using the SDKs for Python, Go, and Node.js, ensuring that our application-specific KPIs were visible in the Collector's logs or exporter output. By the end of the chapter, we achieved confidence in both automated and manual approaches to instrumentation, successfully tracking critical business operations and technical signals in real time, regardless of language or deployment model.

Chapter 5: Telemetry with Attributes and Resource Detectors

Overview

This chapter is going to focus on making telemetry better so that traces, metrics, and logs have strong environmental and platform context. We'll learn how to standardize signals using OpenTelemetry semantic conventions, so that HTTP requests, database queries, and messaging operations follow consistent attribute naming across all services. Next, we'll enable environment and process resource detectors to automatically attach host and runtime details. The idea is that this will help us understand which machines and processes produced each signal. After that, we'll turn on cloud resource detection, focusing on AWS. It'll let telemetry include cloud account, region, and infrastructure identifiers without manual tagging.

The chapter will also cover Kubernetes attribute enrichment, where we'll configure the Collector to attach cluster, namespace, pod, and container metadata to every signal coming from Kubernetes workloads. By the time we're done with this chapter, we'll have telemetry that clearly shows how applications behave, the infrastructure they're running on, and the metadata for the platform.

Applying Semantic Conventions to Signals

When we work with telemetry data, it is easy for signals to become messy if every team, framework, or language chooses different attribute names. The search for HTTP errors or database calls across services becomes frustrating when some signals use **`route`**, others use **`url`**, or a database span is missing a **`db.system`** tag. So here, we need a clear, shared language so that every signal, no matter where it came from, looks familiar and can be filtered, grouped, or analyzed together.

In the following, we will look at practical, hands-on steps to apply semantic conventions for the most common categories, HTTP, database, and messaging signals.

Adding Semantic Conventions for HTTP Signals

I'll use a Python web application as an example. So here, when a request hits our server, we want to record details about the method, route, and status code in a standard way.

For this, inside our handler, we will create a span like the following:

```
with tracer.start_as_current_span(
    "GET /orders/{id}",
    kind=SpanKind.SERVER,
    attributes={
        "http.method": "GET",
```

```
        "http.route": "/orders/{id}",
        "http.status_code": 200,
        "http.target": request.url,
        "http.user_agent": request.headers.get("User-Agent",
""),
    }
) as span:
    # ...business logic...
    pass
```

Now, whenever someone inspects this span, whether in a log, a dashboard, or a trace, they see those same HTTP attributes, every time.

Standardizing Database Attributes

For database operations, we will tag each query with details about the system, database name, and the operation being performed.

```
ctx, span := tracer.Start(ctx, "SELECT orders",
    trace.WithAttributes(
        attribute.String("db.system", "postgresql"),
        attribute.String("db.name", "inventory"),
        attribute.String("db.user", "app_user"),
        attribute.String("db.statement", "SELECT * FROM orders
WHERE id = $1"),
        attribute.String("db.operation", "SELECT"),
    ),
)
defer span.End()
```

The result is that, all the database spanning across the infrastructure make use of the same keys. It thereby makes the dashboards and queries much easier to build.

Tagging Messaging Signals

So here, let us assume that we are consuming messages from Kafka in Node.js. We can instrument the message handler like the following:

```
const span = tracer.startSpan('receive order', {
  kind: 1, // SpanKind.CONSUMER
  attributes: {
    'messaging.system': 'kafka',
    'messaging.destination': 'order-events',
    'messaging.operation': 'process',
    'messaging.message_id': message.id,
  },
});
// ...message processing...
span.end();
```

This ensures that whenever you search for events or measure queue lag, the attributes are named consistently.

Adding Attributes Automatically in Collector

There can be cases wherein not every service sets the tags perfectly. In such a case, we can patch missing attributes using the Collector's attribute processor:

```
processors:
  attributes/set_http_defaults:
    actions:
      - key: http.flavor
        action: insert
        value: "1.1"
service:
  pipelines:
    traces:
      receivers: [otlp]
      processors: [attributes/set_http_defaults]
```

```
      exporters: [logging]
```

Now here, even if an application misses a tag, the Collector can fill in the gaps for us.

By sticking to semantic conventions, we give every tool, dashboard, and teammate the same language for signals, making it easier to troubleshoot, visualize, and optimize our systems, no matter how big our stack becomes.

Use of Environment and Process Resource Detectors

After signals are collected and tagged with semantic conventions, they often lack enough host or process context to quickly answer questions like: Any idea which server this trace came from? What container or process was responsible for this metric?

So, if we don't add info about the environment they're running in to our signals, troubleshooting can be slow, and dashboards won't have meaningful groupings. To close this gap, we need to attach hostnames, container IDs, process IDs, and similar resource attributes to every signal, ideally with minimal manual configuration.

The OpenTelemetry resource detectors can automatically gather and inject host, process, and environment metadata into every span, metric, and log. These detectors are enabled in our SDK code or in the Collector configuration, so resource attributes like host.name, process.pid, or container details show up with each signal. Once enabled, we check that these new attributes are present by reviewing the Collector's output or our backend's trace and metric views.

So, in this recipe, we will walk through enabling environment and process resource detectors for Python, Go, and Node.js, and then verify their effect in the Collector.

Enabling Resource Detectors in Python

When initializing the SDK, we can activate built-in detectors that automatically gather host and process metadata. Following is how we set it up:

```
from opentelemetry.sdk.resources import Resource,
get_aggregated_resources

from opentelemetry.sdk.resources import
ProcessResourceDetector, EnvironmentResourceDetector,
HostResourceDetector

detectors = [ProcessResourceDetector(),
EnvironmentResourceDetector(), HostResourceDetector()]
```

```
resource =
get_aggregated_resources(detector_iterable=detectors)
from opentelemetry.sdk.trace import TracerProvider
from opentelemetry.sdk.trace.export import BatchSpanProcessor
from opentelemetry.exporter.otlp.proto.grpc.trace_exporter
import OTLPSpanExporter
from opentelemetry import trace
trace.set_tracer_provider(
    TracerProvider(resource=resource)
)
exporter = OTLPSpanExporter(endpoint="localhost:4317",
insecure=True)
span_processor = BatchSpanProcessor(exporter)
trace.get_tracer_provider().add_span_processor(span_processor)
```

This will attach metadata like **`host.name`**, **`process.pid`**, and any environment variables to every exported span.

Enabling Resource Detectors in Go

The OpenTelemetry Go SDK supports resource detectors through the resource provider setup:

```
import (
    "go.opentelemetry.io/otel/sdk/resource"
    "go.opentelemetry.io/otel/sdk/resource/process"
    "go.opentelemetry.io/otel/sdk/resource/host"
    "context"
)
res, _ := resource.New(context.Background(),
    resource.WithDetectors(
        process.NewDetector(),
        host.NewDetector(),
    ),
```

```
)
tp := sdktrace.NewTracerProvider(
    sdktrace.WithResource(res),
    // ... other options ...
)
```

Now, each trace, metric, or log sent from this Go app includes host and process info.

Enabling Resource Detectors in Node.js

For Node.js, the resource detectors are included in the SDK configuration:

```
const { NodeSDK } = require('@opentelemetry/sdk-node');
const { hostDetector, processDetector, envDetector } =
require('@opentelemetry/resource-detector');
const sdk = new NodeSDK({
  resourceDetectors: [hostDetector, processDetector,
envDetector],
  // ...other SDK options...
});
sdk.start();
```

The signals emitted from the Node.js app will now be enriched with host and process attributes.

Verifying Resource Attributes

After enabling resource detectors, we then run our instrumented application and then review the output in the Collector's logs or our telemetry backend. So here, in the logging exporter, we should see new resource fields such as:

```
Resource:
    host.name: "webserver-01"
    process.pid: 1425
    process.executable.name: "python3"
    process.runtime.version: "3.10.12"
    os.type: "linux"
```

```
container.id: "d17e0a4d62..."
```

If using a dashboard or Jaeger, these attributes will appear as filterable tags or columns.

Overall, we were able to automatically enrich every signal with host and runtime context. It made far easier to filter, diagnose, and correlate telemetry by server, process, or environment, and closing the loop on full-stack observability.

Enabling Cloud Resource Detectors

Let's say we've spent time setting up resource detectors for the host and process, but when a span arrives in our backend, we can't tell which AWS account, region, or VM sent it. It makes triage tricky. What we want is for the Collector or SDK to automatically tag every span and metric with AWS details. That way, in production, we always know the cloud resource for every signal.

For most teams, enabling cloud detection in the SDK is easiest, especially when deploying Python, Go, or Node.js apps into AWS. In this recipe, we will use Python for this walkthrough, and the concept is similar for Go and Node.js.

Activate AWS Resource Detector

At first, inside our Python application, right at the point where we set up our tracer provider, we add the AWS detectors:

```
from opentelemetry.sdk.resources import Resource,
get_aggregated_resources

from opentelemetry.sdk.resources import
AwsEc2ResourceDetector, AwsEcsResourceDetector,
EnvironmentResourceDetector

# Aggregate AWS and environment detectors

detectors = [AwsEc2ResourceDetector(),
AwsEcsResourceDetector(), EnvironmentResourceDetector()]

resource =
get_aggregated_resources(detector_iterable=detectors)

from opentelemetry.sdk.trace import TracerProvider

from opentelemetry.exporter.otlp.proto.grpc.trace_exporter
import OTLPSpanExporter

from opentelemetry.sdk.trace.export import BatchSpanProcessor

from opentelemetry import trace
```

```
trace.set_tracer_provider(TracerProvider(resource=resource))

exporter = OTLPSpanExporter(endpoint="localhost:4317",
insecure=True)

trace.get_tracer_provider().add_span_processor(BatchSpanProces
sor(exporter))
```

With this, when our app runs inside AWS, the OpenTelemetry will reach out to AWS instance metadata endpoints and grab context about the VM or container.

Enrichment Confirmation

After deploying the instrumented app on an AWS instance (or container), we need to trigger some requests so telemetry is emitted. So here, we will open the OpenTelemetry Collector logs or our tracing backend, and inspect a trace or metric.

We want to see new resource fields such as:

- **`cloud.provider: "aws"`**
- **`cloud.account.id: "123456789012"`**
- **`cloud.region: "us-west-2"`**
- **`host.id: "i-0abc123456def"`**
- **`aws.ecs.cluster.arn: "arn:aws:ecs:..."`**

All the above tags are automatically fetched, if we see them. And then, our AWS resource detector is working. If these tags do not show up, we then must double-check that the instance or container role has access to the AWS instance metadata endpoint and that there are no firewall rules blocking the metadata service.

In Go, we use the AWS detector from the OpenTelemetry contrib package and plug it into our resource aggregation when building the tracer provider. And, in Node.js, we add the AWS resource detectors to the **`resourceDetectors`** array in the NodeSDK config and start as usual.

Now, every trace, metric, or log emitted from our application carries rich AWS context, cloud provider, account, region, and IDs, without us needing to hard-code anything or update config for each new deployment. This makes our telemetry instantly more actionable and our dashboards, filters, and alerts much smarter for cloud-native production operations.

Enhancing Kubernetes Attribute

When we run services inside Kubernetes, knowing that a trace came from "**`app-server-1`**" or "**`api-deployment-5fd8b6fd78-2xkbr`**" is far more helpful than just seeing a generic host or process name. If we want to investigate issues, debug deployment errors, or group metrics by cluster, pod, or namespace, our telemetry must include those details.

So here, we need to following the following simple steps:

Enable Kubernetes Resource Detection

For most real-world Kubernetes environments, the OpenTelemetry Collector is deployed as a DaemonSet, running on every node, as learned in the initial chapters. The Collector can automatically discover and attach Kubernetes context to each signal it handles by enabling the Kubernetes resource detector.

So here, we will edit the Collector configuration and enable the **k8sattributes** processor. This processor will talk to the Kubernetes API and extracts details like cluster name, pod, namespace, container, and node info.

To begin with, we will first add the processor section:

```
processors:
  k8sattributes:
    auth_type: serviceAccount
    extract:
      metadata:
        - k8s.namespace.name
        - k8s.pod.name
        - k8s.pod.uid
        - k8s.node.name
        - k8s.cluster.name
        - k8s.container.name
```

In the above, the **auth_type: serviceAccount** line then uses the pod's own credentials to query the Kubernetes API, which is the usual way when running in a cluster.

Wire Processor into Pipelines

Next, we then reference the **k8sattributes** processor in our signal pipelines. Following is how we would update a traces pipeline:

```
service:
  pipelines:
```

```
    traces:
      receivers: [otlp]
      processors: [k8sattributes]
      exporters: [logging]
```

In the similar way, we can do for **metrics** and **logs** pipelines.

Apply Config and Validate Telemetry

After saving the config, we roll out the changes by restarting the Collector pods. In Kubernetes, this usually means restarting the DaemonSet or reapplying the deployment.

```
kubectl rollout restart daemonset <collector-daemonset-name> -
n <namespace>
```

After this, we then interact with our app running in Kubernetes to emit some traces or metrics. In the Collector's logging exporter or in our backend, we examine the resource section of a new span, metric, or log.

We should now see Kubernetes tags such as:

- **k8s.cluster.name: "production-cluster"**
- **k8s.namespace.name: "order-system"**
- **k8s.pod.name: "api-deployment-5fd8b6fd78-2xkbr"**
- **k8s.pod.uid: "0c0b8fdc-..."**
- **k8s.node.name: "gke-cluster-node-1"**
- **k8s.container.name: "order-api"**

All these above ones are attached automatically to every telemetry signal that the Collector processes on that node. If any of these are missing, we check that the Collector has the right RBAC permissions to read Kubernetes metadata and that it is running with the necessary environment variables.

Summary

Overall, we focused on enriching telemetry so that every signal carried meaningful and consistent context. We applied OpenTelemetry semantic conventions to standardize attributes for HTTP, database, and messaging operations, which ensured that traces and metrics followed a shared vocabulary across services and languages. We then enabled environment and process resource detectors, allowing host-level and runtime metadata such as hostname, process ID, runtime version, and operating system details to be attached automatically to signals.

Later, we then activated cloud resource detection for AWS, which enriched telemetry with cloud-specific context like account ID, region, instance identifiers, and container metadata when workloads ran on EC2 or ECS. Finally, we configured Kubernetes attribute enrichment in the Collector, enabling automatic capture of cluster, namespace, pod, node, and container information for workloads running inside Kubernetes. Throughout the chapter, we validated each enrichment step by reviewing Collector output and backend views, confirming that new resource attributes appeared consistently on traces, metrics, and logs.

CHAPTER 6: ADVANCED SIGNAL PROCESSING AND FILTERING

Overview

In this chapter, we will focus on advanced techniques to process, filter, and enrich the telemetry signals flowing through our OpenTelemetry Collector pipelines. We will begin by configuring the Collector to accept traces from multiple popular protocols, including OTLP, Jaeger, and Zipkin, so that we can support any application or team, no matter their existing instrumentation. We will learn how to filter and drop noisy or verbose spans and logs right at the pipeline level, keeping our observability data lean and relevant.

Next, we will demonstrate how to collect both host-level and application-level metrics simultaneously, ensuring a complete picture of system and service health. Finally, we will explore ways to surface hidden business context by extracting baggage items into span attributes, making it easier to correlate and search for critical user or tenant information.

Configuring Receivers for OTLP, Jaeger, and Zipkin

Our infrastructure very oftenly includes services instrumented at different times, with various teams using the protocol they found most convenient. And, if the OpenTelemetry Collector listens only for OTLP, traces from applications sending via Jaeger or Zipkin will never make it to our observability stack. This leads to gaps in our traces, making it much harder to get a unified view of requests as they flow across services.

So here, we need to enable and validate all major receivers so our pipelines remain future-proof and inclusive. For this, we will update our Collector configuration to activate the Jaeger and Zipkin receivers alongside OTLP. Each receiver listens on its default port and understands its own wire format. We will wire all receivers into the traces pipeline, so no matter which protocol is used upstream, every trace finds its way into our processing flow. After setup, we will test each receiver by sending sample traces to each endpoint and verifying that the Collector processes and logs the incoming data.

Let us work through the hands-on steps together.

Enable Multiple Receivers

We start by editing the **`config.yaml`** file for our Collector. Under the **`receivers`** section, we will add entries for OTLP, Jaeger, and Zipkin. Following is a sample configuration that you can adapt for the environment:

```
receivers:
  otlp:
```

```
    protocols:
      grpc:
        endpoint: 0.0.0.0:4317
      http:
        endpoint: 0.0.0.0:4318
  jaeger:
    protocols:
      grpc:
        endpoint: 0.0.0.0:14250
      thrift_http:
        endpoint: 0.0.0.0:14268
      thrift_compact:
        endpoint: 0.0.0.0:6831
      thrift_binary:
        endpoint: 0.0.0.0:6832
  zipkin:
    endpoint: 0.0.0.0:9411
```

In the above,

- The OTLP receiver listens for both gRPC and HTTP traffic on their standard ports.
- The Jaeger receiver is set to accept traces from any Jaeger agent or client, using all four supported protocols. And,
- The Zipkin receiver listens for HTTP POSTs to port 9411.

Connect Receivers to Traces Pipeline

Under the **service** section, we can wire all three receivers into the same traces pipeline. It ensures any incoming trace, no matter the format, enters the same processing and exporting path:

```
service:
  pipelines:
    traces:
      receivers: [otlp, jaeger, zipkin]
```

```
    processors: [batch]
    exporters: [logging]
```

In the above, we are using a simple batch processor and send output to the logging exporter for validation.

Testing Endpoints

After saving our configuration, we then must restart the Collector to apply the changes. And then, we will verify that each receiver is working.

For OTLP

Here, we will use a test app or **`otel-cli`** to send a test span to **`localhost:4317`** (gRPC) or **`localhost:4318`** (HTTP).

For Jaeger

In the case of Jaeger, we will use **`jaeger-client`** libraries or CLI tools to send traces to **`localhost:14250`** (gRPC), **`localhost:14268`** (HTTP), **`localhost:6831`** (Thrift Compact), or **`localhost:6832`** (Thrift Binary).

For Zipkin

And finally, for Zipkin, we will make use of **`curl`** or a Zipkin-instrumented app to POST JSON spans to **`http://localhost:9411/api/v2/spans`**.

So, after sending a test trace to each of the receiver, we then check the Collector logs (because the logging exporter is active):

```
sudo journalctl -u otelcol.service
```

We should see trace data appear from each protocol, confirming the Collector is successfully receiving and processing all three formats.

After all these steps, our Collector is now well equipped to accept traces from OTLP, Jaeger, and Zipkin sources, eliminating silos and ensuring a single, unified observability pipeline for every service, no matter which tracing protocol it uses.

Filtering Noisy Spans and Logs

As the time goes, our telemetry environment can become flooded with noisy spans (for example, frequent health checks or routine background tasks) and logs (such as repeated debug or info messages). This "noise" distracts from real issues and slows down root cause analysis. If we do not filter this data out at the Collector, our storage, visualization tools, and even billing can spiral out of control. In such situation, we need to set up pipeline-level filters so only valuable, actionable telemetry passes through, while the noise is suppressed as early as possible.

To do this, we can configure the OpenTelemetry Collector to use filter processors (such as **filter** or **attributes**) in our pipelines. These processors match spans or log records based on attribute values, operation names, log content, or any field we choose, and then either drop or keep records based on our rules. And, we will also set up example filters to drop unwanted spans (for example, with the name "/health") and verbose logs (for example, logs at level "DEBUG"), and then validate our filter by generating test noise and observing the Collector output.

Let us work out as above:

Add Filter Processor to Collector Config

To begin with, we start editing our **config.yaml**. Here, under **processors**, we add a filter processor with conditions for the noisy data we want to drop. Let us assume that we want to drop spans named **/health** or **/metrics** and log records at "DEBUG" level. The configuration would look like as below:

```
processors:
  filter/drop_noise_spans:
    traces:
      span:
        - name == "/health"
        - name == "/metrics"
  filter/drop_debug_logs:
    logs:
      record:
        - attributes["log.severity"] == "DEBUG"
```

This sets up two filters; one for the traces and one for the logs. The first drops spans if their name matches **/health** or **/metrics**. The second drops any log record where the **log.severity** attribute is "DEBUG".

Attach Filters to Pipelines

Next, in the **service.pipelines** section, we then reference the new filters. For a traces pipeline:

```
service:
  pipelines:
    traces:
      receivers: [otlp, jaeger, zipkin]
      processors: [filter/drop_noise_spans, batch]
      exporters: [logging]
    logs:
      receivers: [filelog]
      processors: [filter/drop_debug_logs, batch]
      exporters: [logging]
```

This above code ensures that noisy data is dropped before it ever reaches the batch processor or gets exported.

Generate Test Noise

To know if it is working properly, we can run a small test to our filters by deliberately sending noisy data.

- For traces, we can simply send HTTP requests or synthetic spans with the name **`/health`** or **`/metrics`** using any instrumented app, **`curl`**, or a tracing CLI.
- For logs, we may write log entries at the "DEBUG" level and send them through the filelog receiver.

Now, when you monitor the Collector logs or the backend exporter, and if the filter is working, you will notice that only spans with other names (for example, **`/order`**, **`/payment`**) and logs at higher levels (such as "INFO", "ERROR") appear in the output. The **`/health`** and **`/metrics`** spans, and any "DEBUG" log records, are filtered out and do not propagate further.

You can further refine the filter rules to match real noise in the system, using span attributes, log content, or other metadata.

Collecting Host/App Metrics via Receivers

When troubleshooting a slowdown or outage, we often need to correlate infrastructure health (like CPU or memory spikes) with application-level signals (such as request latency or failure rates). If our Collector is set up to receive only one of these, our observability is incomplete and investigations become guesswork. So here, we want to reliably collect both host and application metrics together, such that there are no gaps between system performance and service behavior.

Now, the OpenTelemetry Collector offers several receivers for metrics:

- The **hostmetrics** receiver collects CPU, memory, filesystem, disk, and network usage from the operating system.
- The **prometheus** or **otlp** receivers capture metrics emitted by our applications (for example, via Prometheus endpoints or OTLP exporters).

If we wire both into the Collector's metrics pipeline, we may bring all the relevant signals into a single flow. And then, we can simply validate the setup by checking for both system-level and application-level metrics in the Collector's output.

We will trial out this approach in the following:

Enable Host and Application Metrics Receivers

At first, we need to open the Collector's **config.yaml** and add both **hostmetrics** and **prometheus** (or **otlp**) receivers:

```
receivers:
  hostmetrics:
    collection_interval: 30s
    scrapers:
      cpu: {}
      memory: {}
      disk: {}
      filesystem: {}
      network: {}
  prometheus:
    config:
      scrape_configs:
        - job_name: 'myapp'
          static_configs:
            - targets: ['localhost:8081']  # Replace with the
app's Prometheus endpoint
  otlp:
```

```
    protocols:
      grpc:
      http:
```

In the above script,

- **hostmetrics** will scrape OS stats every 30 seconds. And,
- **prometheus** will scrape application metrics from any endpoint that exposes a Prometheus-compatible **/metrics** path.

Connect Receivers in Metrics Pipeline

We then need to wire both receivers into the metrics pipeline under **service.pipelines**:

```
service:
  pipelines:
    metrics:
      receivers: [hostmetrics, prometheus, otlp]
      processors: [batch]
      exporters: [logging]
```

This will let the Collector accept metrics from all three sources and send them downstream (for now, to the logging exporter).

Validating Outputs

Now, we will generate activity to produce both host and app metrics:

- We can run a CPU or disk-intensive process on the host to ensure the **hostmetrics** receiver has data to collect.
- Or, we may expose application metrics by making requests to the service or emitting metrics through the Prometheus or OTLP endpoint.

Now, we will review the Collector's logging exporter:

```
sudo journalctl -u otelcol.service
```

In the output, we need to look for lines like:

```
ResourceMetrics #0
```

```
Metric #0
    name: system.cpu.utilization
Metric #1
    name: system.memory.usage
Metric #2
    name: http_requests_total
Metric #3
    name: custom_application_kpi
```

The appearance of both system metrics (CPU, memory, disk, etc.) and application metrics (HTTP requests, custom counters) will confirm us that both receivers are active and working as intended.

If you do not see both, then we must double-check the Collector's permissions, endpoint URLs, and ensure the application is exposing metrics. We can also fine-tune the scrape intervals, or add new endpoints, or we may include more scrapers as needed for full observability.

Extracting Baggage into Spans

We must remember that the distributed traces often carry baggage items, key-value pairs like **user.id**, **tenant**, or **region**, that flow with the context across service calls. And, by default, this baggage is used for propagation and may not appear directly as span attributes in our observability tools. So, when we want to filter or group traces by this business context, we need these baggage items to show up as searchable span fields, not just hidden context. Hence, our aim here is to extract baggage into span attributes at the Collector level, making these details visible wherever our traces are exported.

Now, we know that the OpenTelemetry Collector provides a **baggage** processor that can extract specified baggage keys from each span context and copy them into the span's attributes. So in this recipe, we will configure this processor in our pipeline, define which baggage keys to extract, and then confirm they appear in the trace attributes downstream.

Add Baggage Processor to Collector Config

To begin with, we will first edit the Collector's **config.yaml** to include a baggage processor with the keys you want to extract. For instance, if we want to extract **user.id** and **tenant** baggage items:

```
processors:
  baggage/extract_to_attributes:
```

```
    extract:
      keys:
        - from_key: user.id
          to_attribute: user.id
        - from_key: tenant
          to_attribute: tenant
```

This will tell the Collector to look for **user.id** and **tenant** baggage on each span and turn them into regular span attributes.

Attach Processor to Traces Pipeline

Next, we then wire the processor into the traces pipeline:

```
service:
  pipelines:
    traces:
      receivers: [otlp, jaeger, zipkin]
      processors: [baggage/extract_to_attributes, batch]
      exporters: [logging]
```

It will confirm that the extraction happens for every incoming trace before batching and exporting.

Generate Test Baggage and Validate Output

Now, in the instrumented application, we will then start a span and set baggage keys in the trace context:

```
from opentelemetry import trace, baggage, context
ctx = baggage.set_baggage("user.id", "alice")
ctx = baggage.set_baggage("tenant", "retail", context=ctx)
tracer = trace.get_tracer(__name__)
with tracer.start_as_current_span("process_order",
context=ctx):
    pass
```

After running the app, wee will then check the Collector logs or the trace backend. For each processed span, we should now see new attributes:

```
Attributes:
    user.id: "alice"
    tenant: "retail"
```

These will be present on every span where the baggage was set upstream. It makes easy to filter or group traces by user or tenant.

Summary

To conclude, we explored the further capability of OpenTelemetry's Collector to handle advanced signal processing and filtering. We started by enabling multiple protocol receivers, OTLP, Jaeger, and Zipkin, so that traces from a variety of sources could enter our unified pipeline. We then tackled the challenge of noisy telemetry by configuring filter processors to suppress unwanted spans and verbose log messages, ensuring only valuable data moved downstream.

Next, we brought together host and application metrics by enabling the hostmetrics and Prometheus receivers, validating that both system and service health could be monitored together in real time. To make our business context more accessible, we configured the baggage processor to extract baggage keys like user IDs and tenant names, surfacing them as span attributes for easier search and correlation. Each step was hands-on and validated by generating test telemetry and reviewing the output to confirm our configurations worked as expected. By the end of this chapter, we had built a Collector setup capable of accepting diverse signals, reducing noise, correlating infrastructure and application health, and exposing critical context in every trace for advanced troubleshooting.

CHAPTER 7: OBSERVABILITY IN KUBERNETES

Overview

In this chapter, we're going to focus on building solid observability practices specifically for Kubernetes environments. To start, we'll learn how to set up the OpenTelemetry Collector as a DaemonSet. This'll make sure that telemetry collection runs smoothly on every node in the cluster. Then, we'll switch to a gateway-based deployment model, where we centralize telemetry from across the cluster for processing and export.

After that, we'll enable Kubernetes-specific receivers and processors that attach pod, node, namespace, and cluster metadata to every signal. We'll also set up Prometheus scraping to collect metrics for the whole cluster, so we can keep an eye on infrastructure health, platform behavior, and application performance all at once. Finally, we'll route Kubernetes telemetry to external observability platforms like Grafana and Jaeger, just to make sure that metrics and traces are visible and usable for monitoring and alerting. By the time we're done with this chapter, we'll have a full observability setup for Kubernetes that's all set for production.

Deploying Collector as DaemonSet

The Kubernetes delivers power and flexibility by dynamically scheduling containers across a pool of nodes. This very flexibility, however, creates a unique observability challenge. Now think of a node crashing, a new one joining, or a noisy pod moving between nodes, if our telemetry collection does not adapt just as quickly, we end up with blind spots in our cluster. A single Collector deployment might miss logs from pods scheduled on remote nodes, fail to capture node-level metrics, or become a bottleneck as traffic grows. For full visibility, troubleshooting, and compliance, we must ensure that every node, no matter when it appears or disappears, is always monitored with the same standards and receives immediate coverage.

In this recipe, we will deploy the OpenTelemetry Collector as a DaemonSet by applying a Kubernetes manifest. The manifest will then tell the Kubernetes to create a Collector pod on every node, with a consistent configuration provided via ConfigMap. Once deployed, we will validate our setup by confirming each node has its own Collector pod, and that all pods are healthy and ready to process telemetry.

In the following, we will put this into action as shown below:

Apply DaemonSet Manifest

To begin with, we will first prepare the DaemonSet manifest, this describes how Kubernetes should run the Collector on every node:

```
apiVersion: apps/v1
kind: DaemonSet
```

```yaml
metadata:
  name: otel-collector
  namespace: observability
spec:
  selector:
    matchLabels:
      app: otel-collector
  template:
    metadata:
      labels:
        app: otel-collector
    spec:
      containers:
        - name: otel-collector
          image: otel/opentelemetry-collector:latest
          args: ["--config=/etc/otel-collector-config.yaml"]
          volumeMounts:
            - name: config
              mountPath: /etc/otel-collector-config.yaml
              subPath: otel-collector-config.yaml
      volumes:
        - name: config
          configMap:
            name: otel-collector-config
```

After this, we then apply it to our cluster:

```
kubectl apply -f otel-collector-daemonset.yaml
```

The Kubernetes schedules one Collector pod per node, no matter how many nodes we have now or add in the future.

Validate Pod Distribution and Node Coverage

Next, we then check that each node is running a Collector pod:

```
kubectl get pods -n observability -o wide | grep otel-
collector
```

Here, we should see that every node in the **NODE** column has a corresponding Collector pod.

After this, we must check DaemonSet status to ensure all pods are ready:

```
kubectl get daemonset otel-collector -n observability
```

In the output, the **DESIRED**, **CURRENT**, and **READY** columns should all match the number of nodes in the cluster.

Confirm Collector Health

And finally, we confirm the Collector is working, and for it, we check the logs from any pod:

```
kubectl logs -n observability <otel-collector-pod-name>
```

A healthy startup log generally shows the Collector loaded the config and started listening for signals.

With this setup, every node, every workload, and every transition in the cluster's lifecycle is now instantly covered, setting us up for reliable, scalable, and production-grade monitoring across the entire environment.

Deploying Collector as Gateway

While a DaemonSet provides complete node-level coverage, many observability workflows benefit from centralizing telemetry, routing all signals through one or more dedicated gateway Collectors. Without a gateway, exporting data to an external observability platform from every agent increases egress costs, multiplies configuration drift, and makes policy enforcement harder. So here, we need a way to collect, process, and export telemetry from a central location, exposing clear endpoints for agent or application ingestion, and validating that telemetry is both received and forwarded as intended.

In this solution, we will deploy the OpenTelemetry Collector as a central gateway using a Kubernetes Deployment and Service. And, the agents or application SDKs throughout the cluster will send traces, metrics, and logs to this gateway, which will process the data and export it to external backends.

In the following, we will work upon the gateway deployment, endpoint exposure, and validation together.

Deploy Gateway Collector

At first, we will prepare the Kubernetes manifest for the Collector as a Deployment. This will run one or more replicas in a highly available fashion. Following is an example you can save as **otel-collector-gateway.yaml**:

```
apiVersion: apps/v1
kind: Deployment
metadata:
  name: otel-collector-gateway
  namespace: observability
spec:
  replicas: 2
  selector:
    matchLabels:
      app: otel-collector-gateway
  template:
    metadata:
      labels:
        app: otel-collector-gateway
    spec:
      containers:
        - name: otel-collector
          image: otel/opentelemetry-collector:latest
          args: ["--config=/etc/otel-collector-config.yaml"]
          ports:
            - containerPort: 4317  # OTLP gRPC
            - containerPort: 4318  # OTLP HTTP
          volumeMounts:
```

```
            - name: config
              mountPath: /etc/otel-collector-config.yaml
              subPath: otel-collector-config.yaml
      volumes:
        - name: config
          configMap:
            name: otel-collector-config
```

After this, we then apply the deployment with:

```
kubectl apply -f otel-collector-gateway.yaml
```

Expose Gateway Endpoints

Now, to make the gateway accessible within or outside the cluster, we then expose its ports using a Kubernetes Service. In the following, I am giving you a simple service manifest:

```
apiVersion: v1
kind: Service
metadata:
  name: otel-collector-gateway
  namespace: observability
spec:
  type: ClusterIP
  ports:
    - name: otlp-grpc
      port: 4317
      targetPort: 4317
    - name: otlp-http
      port: 4318
      targetPort: 4318
  selector:
```

```
    app: otel-collector-gateway
```

You then apply it as below:

```
kubectl apply -f otel-collector-gateway-service.yaml
```

After this, the agents and apps in the cluster can now send telemetry to **otel-collector-gateway.observability.svc.cluster.local:4317** (gRPC) or **:4318** (HTTP).

Validate Telemetry Reception and Export

Now, to ensure everything is connected, we will check that the Deployment pods are running:

```
kubectl get pods -n observability -l app=otel-collector-
gateway
```

After this, we then review the logs of a gateway pod for incoming traces or metrics:

```
kubectl logs -n observability <gateway-pod-name>
```

We can also send a test trace or metric from an agent or SDK configured to point at the gateway endpoint. And then we can look for logs indicating that signals are being received and then exported to the downstream backend. All the data flows through a single point, simplifying network security, processing policies, and connection management to any external observability tool. This gateway becomes the anchor for multi-cluster, hybrid cloud, or enterprise-scale OpenTelemetry adoption.

Configuring Kubernetes Receivers for Metadata

When we collect metrics, logs, or traces from applications running in Kubernetes, we often need more than just the raw signal, we need to know exactly where in the cluster it came from. For instance, if a metric spike appears, is it tied to a specific pod, node, or namespace? Are errors happening only on certain deployments? Without this metadata, our dashboards are vague and troubleshooting is much harder. To get full context, we need the Collector to enrich every signal with Kubernetes metadata, linking each piece of telemetry to its real source in the cluster.

So here, the solution is, that we can use the OpenTelemetry Collector's **k8scluster** and **k8sattributes** receivers and processors to automatically pull in Kubernetes metadata for each signal. By doing it like this, every trace, metric, and log is tagged with the pod name, namespace, node, and even cluster name. After this, we will enable these components in our Collector configuration, and then validate by checking that our telemetry shows the correct context tags.

Let us experiment as below:

Enable Kubernetes Receivers and Processors

To start with, in the Collector's **config.yaml**, we will add the **k8scluster** receiver and reference the **k8sattributes** processor:

```
receivers:
  otlp:
    protocols:
      grpc:
      http:
  k8scluster:
    auth_type: serviceAccount
processors:
  k8sattributes:
    auth_type: serviceAccount
    extract:
      metadata:
        - k8s.namespace.name
        - k8s.pod.name
        - k8s.pod.uid
        - k8s.node.name
        - k8s.cluster.name
        - k8s.container.name
```

This will let the Collector to talk to the Kubernetes API using its service account, and thus it will help extracting the most important tags.

Reference in Pipelines

After this, we will then wire the receivers and processors into the pipelines:

```
service:
  pipelines:
```

```
traces:
  receivers: [otlp]
  processors: [k8sattributes, batch]
  exporters: [logging]
metrics:
  receivers: [otlp, k8scluster]
  processors: [k8sattributes, batch]
  exporters: [logging]
logs:
  receivers: [otlp]
  processors: [k8sattributes, batch]
  exporters: [logging]
```

With this, every signal passing through these pipelines will be automatically enriched with Kubernetes metadata.

Validate Metadata Tags in Telemetry

After restarting or redeploying the Collector, we will then generate some telemetry by making requests or triggering metrics in the cluster.

And, to verify, we will check the Collector's logging exporter:

```
kubectl logs -n observability <otel-collector-pod-name>
```

In the output, we then must look for resources and attributes as below:

```
Resource:
    k8s.cluster.name: "production-cluster"
    k8s.namespace.name: "orders"
    k8s.pod.name: "order-api-65d47bcddf-wx5qn"
    k8s.node.name: "gke-node-1"
    k8s.container.name: "order-api"
```

If we see the above tags, then it confirms that our Collector is correctly attaching the pod, node, and cluster context to every signal.

If you do not see the tags, we then must double-check if the Collector's service account has the correct RBAC permissions to access the Kubernetes API and metadata.

Capturing Cluster Telemetry with Prometheus Scraping

While working with Kubernetes, at some point of time, we do feel the pain of missing metrics when diagnosing a cluster-wide problem. This could be a CPU pressure on a node, or a sudden jump in failed pods. But without proper metrics from every corner of the cluster, it is impossible to answer "what just happened?". Also, relying only on application metrics does not cut it, rather we need node stats, kube-system data, and pod-level signals to get a complete story.

To add some importsant info to you, the Prometheus is a suitable standard for scraping such metrics in Kubernetes. So here, we will tap the OpenTelemetry Collector into all that Prometheus data and stream it into our observability pipeline, making sure we not only write the right YAML but also know how to check it is working in our environment.

Setting up Prometheus Receiver

We will add a **`prometheus`** receiver in our config file that will scan for metrics endpoints in the cluster. You just consider this receiver as Prometheus itself, as it can discover, scrape, and collect the metrics from all the places we care about.

The following is the sample configuration which you need to write as it is:

```
receivers:
  prometheus:
    config:
      scrape_configs:
        - job_name: 'kubernetes-nodes'
          kubernetes_sd_configs:
            - role: node
          relabel_configs:
            - action: labelmap
              regex: __meta_kubernetes_node_label_(.+)
        - job_name: 'kubernetes-pods'
          kubernetes_sd_configs:
```

```
        - role: pod
      relabel_configs:
        - action: labelmap
          regex: __meta_kubernetes_pod_label_(.+)
```

In the above,

- The first **job_name** tells the Collector to look for node-level metrics, think node-exporter on every node.
- The second **job_name** points to all pods in the cluster. If our apps (or infra pods) expose a **/metrics** endpoint, the Collector will find and scrape them.

If we run Prometheus exporters like **kube-state-metrics** or node-exporter, we just add more **job_name** blocks, one per exporter or metric source.

Exposing Metrics Endpoints

Now, before the Collector can scrape anything, those endpoints need to exist! If we are unsure, then we simply run the following:

```
kubectl get pods -A -o wide | grep exporter
```

In the output, we want to see pods like **node-exporter**, **kube-state-metrics**, or our own services with metrics ports open.

Hooking up Pipeline

Next, we must connect our receiver to the Collector's metrics pipeline. In the **service** section, we then must specify:

```
service:
  pipelines:
    metrics:
      receivers: [prometheus]
      processors: [batch]
      exporters: [logging]
```

This tells the Collector, that every metric scraped by Prometheus goes through batching and is then exported. For now, we are logging to the console, which is perfect for validation.

Deployment and Validatation

And finally, we then save the YAML, and roll out the Collector:

```
kubectl apply -f <your-collector-config.yaml>
```

After this, we then grab the logs from one of the Collector pods:

```
kubectl logs -n observability <otel-collector-pod-name>
```

In the output, we want to see metrics like **node_cpu_seconds_total**, **kube_pod_info**, **kube_node_status_allocatable_cpu**, and any custom application metrics we emit (for example, **myapp_requests_total**).

If we see these flowing in the logs, we know the Collector is successfully scraping and processing metrics from the whole cluster. If we do not, we then must double-check that the exporters are running and accessible, and that our Collector's service account has the right permissions.

Exporting Kubernetes Telemetry to Observability Backends

Once our OpenTelemetry Collector is collecting traces, metrics, and logs from across our cluster, our next challenge is to deliver these signals to external backends where we can use them. If we leave telemetry stranded inside the cluster, or only export logs, we miss out on dashboards, distributed traces, and real-time alerting. We are required to route their telemetry to Grafana, Jaeger, or any chosen platform, such that it is always accessible for visualization, correlation, and automated monitoring.

So, the solution is that, we will configure the Collector's exporters for both traces and metrics, and then we will connect each pipeline, set the target backend endpoints, and then validate end-to-end by viewing data in Grafana and Jaeger. This confirms that every signal travels from the Kubernetes cluster directly to the tools we trust for operations and analysis.

In the following, we will start to wire up our pipelines:

Configuring Exporters in Collector

We first add the exporters for both Jaeger and Prometheus. This is because the Grafana often uses Prometheus as a metrics source:

```
exporters:
  jaeger:
```

```
    endpoint: "jaeger-
collector.observability.svc.cluster.local:14250"
    tls:
      insecure: true
  prometheusremotewrite:
    endpoint: "http://prometheus-
server.observability.svc.cluster.local:9090/api/v1/write"
  otlp:
    endpoint: "grafana-
agent.observability.svc.cluster.local:4317"
    tls:
      insecure: true
```

Just to make understanding easy, in the above:

- The **jaeger** exporter routes traces to the Jaeger backend.
- The **prometheusremotewrite** exporter sends metrics to a Prometheus-compatible backend. And,
- The **otlp** exporter is available for targets supporting the OTLP protocol.

Connect Pipelines to Exporters

Next, we then wire the appropriate pipelines to their exporters:

```
service:
  pipelines:
    traces:
      receivers: [otlp, jaeger]
      processors: [k8sattributes, batch]
      exporters: [jaeger]
    metrics:
      receivers: [prometheus]
      processors: [k8sattributes, batch]
      exporters: [prometheusremotewrite]
```

Here, we can also use multiple exporters per pipeline if needed. It makes possible the routing of same signals to more than one backend.

Testing with Grafana and Jaeger

Now, we will verify our setup end-to-end:

For Jaeger (traces)

We will first open Jaeger's web UI, and then we will trigger some traces in the applications (for example, make API requests).

In the Jaeger UI, we will then search for the service name. here, we should see new traces, complete with Kubernetes metadata as attributes on each span.

For Grafana (metrics)

We will add Prometheus as a data source within Grafana. And then, we will explore the various dashboards or we can also run queries such as:

```
node_cpu_seconds_total

kube_pod_info

http_requests_total
```

From the above queries, we should see live data flowing from the cluster, reflecting node, pod, and app metrics. If the data does not appear, we then must check the Collector logs for exporter errors and confirm network connectivity and correct endpoint URLs for each backend.

Summary

To sum up, we worked through establishing full observability for Kubernetes environments. We deployed the Collector as a DaemonSet to ensure every node was covered, guaranteeing local access to node-level signals and consistent telemetry collection even as nodes scaled up or down. We then introduced the gateway deployment model, centralizing telemetry reception and export to simplify configuration, reduce egress complexity, and create a stable ingestion point for the cluster.

After that, we enabled Kubernetes receivers and processors to enrich signals with pod, namespace, node, and cluster metadata, allowing us to clearly associate telemetry with the exact Kubernetes resources that produced it. We also configured Prometheus scraping to collect cluster-wide metrics, bringing in node, pod, and platform metrics alongside application metrics for unified visibility. Finally, we routed Kubernetes telemetry to external observability platforms by configuring exporters and validating traces in Jaeger and metrics in Grafana. By the end of the chapter, our Kubernetes telemetry flowed reliably from workloads and infrastructure through the Collector and into visualization and alerting systems. It was providing a complete, contextual view of cluster behavior.

Chapter 8: Integrations with Cloud and Observability Platforms

Overview

In this chapter, we're going to learn how to expand our observability pipelines by integrating OpenTelemetry with major cloud and observability platforms used in production environments. The plan is to set up the Collector so it can send signals to AWS CloudWatch and X-Ray. This way, we can make sure our metrics and traces are there in the native AWS consoles for monitoring and alerting.

After that, we'll dive into how to stream OpenTelemetry data into Elastic APM and Elasticsearch for some advanced search, visualization, and analytics. Next, we'll link our pipelines to the Grafana stack, Tempo, Loki, and Prometheus so we can view traces, logs, and metrics in a unified Grafana dashboard. We'll also go over setting up exporters for Splunk, Datadog, and New Relic, making sure all signals are routed to these platforms for real-time analysis and automated alerting. When we do, we'll walk through exporter configuration, credential management, and validation within each backend's UI. This will help us build confidence that our telemetry is truly end-to-end.

Integrating with AWS CloudWatch and X-Ray

As organizations migrate their workloads to AWS, the cloud platform itself becomes the backbone for not only hosting applications, but also for running all operational tooling, monitoring, alerting, and distributed tracing included. Most teams rely heavily on AWS-native services like CloudWatch and X-Ray for their dashboards, alarms, cost management, and deep-dive trace analysis. However, a common pain arises when telemetry generated by our microservices, Kubernetes clusters, or VM-based workloads does not show up in these AWS-native consoles. This disconnect leads to gaps in visibility, siloed troubleshooting, and the loss of automated cloud-native alerting and analytics.

The challenge is even greater when multiple data sources, Kubernetes, EC2, Lambda, and even on-premises nodes, need to present a unified view inside AWS. Without direct integration, teams find themselves with traces in one tool, metrics in another, and alerts in yet another, making root-cause analysis much slower and increasing operational risk. So here, in this recipe, we will use the official AWS exporters provided by the OpenTelemetry Collector to route both metrics and traces into CloudWatch and X-Ray. And, by wiring our Collector pipelines to these exporters and securing access with the correct IAM roles, we can guarantee that every service, whether containerized, serverless, or VM-based, is able to feed the telemetry straight into the AWS platform.

In the following, we will walk through this process and make sure that each of the part works as we desired to.

Add AWS Exporters to Collector Configuration

To begin with, we will first add both the CloudWatch and X-Ray exporters:

```
exporters:
  awsemf:
    region: us-east-1
    namespace: "my-service"
  awsxray:
    region: us-east-1
```

Here,

- The **awsemf** exporter is used for metrics (Amazon CloudWatch Embedded Metric Format).
- The **awsxray** exporter is used for traces.

And, we must ensure that the **region** field matches the deployment region.

Attach Exporters to Pipelines

Next, we then wire these exporters into the Collector's pipelines as shown below:

```
service:
  pipelines:
    metrics:
      receivers: [prometheus, otlp]
      processors: [batch]
      exporters: [awsemf]
    traces:
      receivers: [otlp, jaeger, zipkin]
      processors: [batch]
      exporters: [awsxray]
```

By doing as above, any metrics from Prometheus, OTLP, or other sources gets succerssfully routed to CloudWatch, while the traces are sent to X-Ray.

Provide AWS Credentials to Collector

The Collector must have permission to write to CloudWatch and X-Ray. And, the preferred approach is to run the Collector in an AWS environment with an appropriate IAM role attached (for example, an EC2 instance, ECS task, or EKS service account). The required permissions include:

- **`cloudwatch:PutMetricData`**
- **`xray:PutTraceSegments`**
- **`xray:PutTelemetryRecords`**

And then, for Kubernetes, we will map the role to the Collector service account using IRSA (IAM Roles for Service Accounts).

Deploy in AWS Consoles

After updating and rolling out the Collector, we then head to the AWS consoles:

CloudWatch Console

Here, you first go to CloudWatch, select the right region, and navigate to Metrics. And then, under the namespace you set (for example, "my-service"), and then you should see incoming metrics from the Collector.

X-Ray Console

For AWS X-Ray, open it and search for the service name, and look for new traces or segments appearing in the service map and trace list. If metrics and traces show up as expected, the integration is successful. If not, check Collector logs for export errors and verify that the IAM role or credentials are correct and active.

All the above steps establish a reliable bridge from our OpenTelemetry pipeline directly into AWS CloudWatch and X-Ray. And thereby, it let us use AWS-native dashboards, alerts, and trace search to monitor, investigate, and optimize every part of our cloud-native workloads.

Integrating with Elastic APM and Elasticsearch

It is widely known that many organizations prefer to select Elastic as their powerful unified observability, traces, metrics, and logs searchable in one place, with advanced alerting, dashboards, and analytics. However, by default, the data collected via OpenTelemetry does not automatically show up in the Elastic APM or Kibana dashboards. If we do not stream OTel signals into the Elastic stack, the teams end up with fragmented insights and cannot fully use Elastic's advanced capabilities for troubleshooting or monitoring business health. Hence, to unify the telemetry, we need to export traces and metrics from the Collector directly into Elastic's APM Server and Elasticsearch, and then we can verify that our signals appear where they are needed most.

So, let us begin. The OpenTelemetry Collector provides official exporters for Elastic APM. By configuring these exporters and wiring them into our pipelines, we can send traces and metrics straight to the APM Server and Elasticsearch. Once configured, we will generate test traffic and check the Elastic dashboards for live telemetry, confirming that our setup is delivering full-stack visibility.

Enable Elastic Exporters in Collector

We will firstl add the Elastic exporter:

```
exporters:
  elasticapm:
    server_url: "http://elastic-apm-server.elastic-system.svc.cluster.local:8200"
    secret_token: "your_apm_secret_token"
    api_key: "your_elastic_api_key"  # Optional: use either secret_token or api_key
```

Here,

- **server_url** should point to the Elastic APM Server's service endpoint.
- And, we need to use either a **secret_token** or an **api_key** for authentication.

Wire Exporter into Pipelines

Next, we then connect the traces and metrics pipelines to the exporter:

```
service:
  pipelines:
    traces:
      receivers: [otlp, jaeger, zipkin]
      processors: [batch]
      exporters: [elasticapm]
    metrics:
      receivers: [otlp, prometheus]
      processors: [batch]
      exporters: [elasticapm]
```

This ensures, that all incoming OTel traces and metrics are routed to the Elastic APM Server.

Test Data Flow in Dashboards

After adding the credentials to the server, we then generate test telemetry by making API requests, running sample apps, and using tracing/metrics tools pointed at the Collector.

- In Kibana, we just open the **APM** section and check the list of services for the app or service name.
- Explore traces, transactions, and error details to confirm visibility.
- In **Observability > Metrics**, we must search for the application or cluster metrics.
- You should see live traces, spans, and metrics streaming in.

If data is missing, we can just check the Collector logs for errors, and ensure that the network connectivity to the APM Server, and confirm the credentials.

This recipe generally unlocks the full power of Elastic's search, visualization, and alerting for every trace and metric generated across our distributed systems.

Integrating with Grafana Tempo, Loki, and Prometheus

Once we've collected traces, metrics, and logs with OpenTelemetry, we usually want to visualize and correlate these signals in Grafana, which is designed to query multiple backends at once. But if you don't export telemetry from the Collector to Tempo, Loki, and Prometheus, our dashboards stay empty, traces can't be searched, and log correlation is out of the question. We need a way to connect our OpenTelemetry pipelines directly to these Grafana-managed storage and query platforms. That way, every signal, no matter where it comes from, will go to the right place and can be explored in real time.

The OpenTelemetry Collector provides official exporters for each platform:

- **`otlp`** or **`tempo`** exporter for traces to Tempo
- **`loki`** exporter for logs to Loki
- **`prometheusremotewrite`** exporter for metrics to Prometheus (or compatible systems)

So, in this recipe, we will configure and enable each exporter, route our pipelines accordingly, and then validate by viewing the results in Grafana dashboards. Following is the step-by-step process:

Configure Exporters

In the Collector's **`config.yaml`**, we at first add exporters for Tempo, Loki, and Prometheus:

```
exporters:
  otlp/tempo:
    endpoint: tempo.observability.svc.cluster.local:4317
    tls:
      insecure: true
  loki:
    endpoint:
http://loki.observability.svc.cluster.local:3100/loki/api/v1/p
ush
  prometheusremotewrite:
    endpoint: http://prometheus-
server.observability.svc.cluster.local:9090/api/v1/write
```

Here,

- The **otlp/tempo** exporter sends traces to Tempo over OTLP/gRPC.
- The **loki** exporter pushes logs to Loki using its HTTP API.
- The **prometheusremotewrite** exporter streams metrics to Prometheus.

Connect Exporters to Pipelines

Then, we wire up each exporter in the **service.pipelines** section:

```
service:
  pipelines:
    traces:
      receivers: [otlp, jaeger, zipkin]
      processors: [batch]
      exporters: [otlp/tempo]
    logs:
      receivers: [filelog, otlp]
      processors: [batch]
      exporters: [loki]
    metrics:
```

```
      receivers: [prometheus, otlp]
      processors: [batch]
      exporters: [prometheusremotewrite]
```

With the above configuration, all signals flow from the Collector directly into the Grafana ecosystem.

Validate in Grafana Dashboards

Once the Collector is running with the new exporters, we then do the validation as below for each of the exporters:

Tempo (Traces)

Within the Grafana, we select the Tempo data source, and search for recent traces by service name or tags. We then trigger some requests in the applications and then we watch for new traces to appear.

Loki (Logs)

In Grafana's Explore tab, we choose the Loki data source and search for logs by label (for example, **`job`**, **`app`**, **`namespace`**). And then, we generate log events from the app or test pod to verify ingestion.

Prometheus (Metrics)

Within the Metrics tab, we first select the Prometheus, and then we query for metrics like **`http_requests_total`**, **`process_cpu_seconds_total`**, or any custom metric the services emit.

If all signals show up and can be queried, the pipelines are working perfectly. If anything is missing, we then must check with the Collector logs for exporter errors. Or else, we need to confirm the network connectivity or with the credentials if they are correctly set.

Integrating with Splunk, Datadog, and New Relic

Let's say we've got our OpenTelemetry pipelines collecting traces, metrics, and logs from every corner of our environment, and our teams rely on Splunk, Datadog, or New Relic for their day-to-day monitoring, alerting, and dashboards. If telemetry doesn't reach these SaaS platforms, it's almost like it doesn't exist. That means alerts are being missed, dashboards stay blank, and engineers waste time switching tools. We've got to get our data streaming from the Collector into these platforms, making it instantly visible, searchable, and actionable.

In the following, we will make each connection, as if we are building this in our own system.

Enabling Exporter

We will start with Splunk. Splunk loves logs but can also handle traces and metrics. Here, we need to grab our HEC (HTTP Event Collector) endpoint and a secure token from the Splunk UI.

Within the collector config:

```
exporters:
  splunk_hec:
    token: "<your_splunk_hec_token>"
    endpoint: "https://splunk-hec.example.com:8088"
    source: "otel-collector"
    sourcetype: "_json"
    index: "main"
    insecure_skip_verify: true
```

Next is the Datadog. Here, we fetch our API key from the Datadog UI.

```
exporters:
  datadog:
    api:
      key: "<your_datadog_api_key>"
    metrics:
      endpoint: "https://api.datadoghq.com/api/v1/series"
    traces:
      endpoint: "https://trace.agent.datadoghq.com"
```

And finally for New Relic we get an API key from the New Relic portal.

```
exporters:
  newrelic:
    api_key: "<your_newrelic_api_key>"
```

```
    region: "US"
```

Each of the exporter requires the correct token and network access. If the cluster is behind a firewall, then we have to make sure that the egress is allowed to these SaaS endpoints.

Attaching Exporters to Pipelines

And this is the step where we tie all together. In the **service.pipelines** section, we then specify exactly which data goes where.

Here, we configure to send traces, metrics, and logs everywhere for testing:

```
service:
  pipelines:
    traces:
      receivers: [otlp, jaeger, zipkin]
      processors: [batch]
      exporters: [splunk_hec, datadog, newrelic]
    metrics:
      receivers: [prometheus, otlp]
      processors: [batch]
      exporters: [splunk_hec, datadog, newrelic]
    logs:
      receivers: [filelog, otlp]
      processors: [batch]
      exporters: [splunk_hec]
```

This exporter attachment can be refined as we like. It could be just logs go to Splunk, traces to New Relic, and metrics to Datadog, depending on our needs.

Deploy and Generate Test Data

We then roll out the Collector update as below:

```
kubectl apply -f otel-collector-config.yaml
```

We can like that create some telemetry:

- We will trigger a few API calls in the services (for traces and logs)
- And then, we will generate metrics by running a load test or just interacting with the application

Validation in Platform's UI

Splunk

In splunk, first open the Splunk Search and Reporting UI. This is where we can search through all the incoming data. At the top, we will find a search bar. Here, let us enter a search query that targets our specific data. For example, if we want to see data collected by OpenTelemetry, we might type something like **`index=main sourcetype=_json source=otel-collector`**. This query tells Splunk to look in the main index, filter for entries with the sourcetype _json, and only show results where the source is set to otel-collector.

As soon as we run this query, the Splunk should start displaying fresh log and trace events that match our filters. These events usually appear in real time, so we can monitor what is happening almost immediately after data is sent. If we do not see any results or if we expect more data than is shown, it is a good idea to check the logs from the OpenTelemetry Collector itself.

Datadog

In the search bar on the APM dashboard, we will enter the name of the service we expect to see traces from. If traces are not showing up right away, we can trigger an action in our application that should result in a trace, such as sending a request or running a specific transaction. As soon as the trace is generated, it should appear in the traces list in Datadog. Watching for it helps us verify end-to-end connectivity from the application to Datadog.

Beyond traces, Datadog also offers dashboards for system and application metrics. We can open the Infrastructure section or the Metrics Explorer to see if our host and application metrics are arriving as expected. These views provide a wealth of information, from CPU and memory usage to custom business metrics.

New Relic

In New Relic, we start by logging into the New Relic One interface. It acts as the main hub for all observability data. In the main menu, we choose "APM & Services." This area lets us search for and select the application or service we are monitoring.

Upon selecting the desired service, we can review incoming traces and metrics. New Relic provides graphical views of request traces, error rates, and performance metrics. If the setup is working correctly, we should see recent data populating these dashboards, confirming that our integration is successful.

With all these integrations live and validated, we have put our telemetry right where our teams expect it. Every span, metric, and log now light up dashboards, triggers alerts, and powers search and analytics in Splunk, Datadog, and New Relic. This step is where observability goes from theory to real impact, no more silos, no more blind spots, just real-time, actionable data for every corner of our stack.

Summary

As we went through this chapter, we learned to link our OpenTelemetry pipelines with top cloud and observability platforms. We started by linking the Collector with AWS CloudWatch and X-Ray, setting up exporters, and checking that metrics and traces showed up in the AWS consoles. Then, we set up connections to Elastic APM and Elasticsearch, which lets us stream OTel data into Elastic's awesome dashboards and search tools. Then, we moved to the Grafana stack, wiring our pipelines to Tempo for traces, Loki for logs, and Prometheus for metrics. We validated this integration by exploring live data in Grafana dashboards. We finally got our Collector hooked up to Splunk, Datadog, and New Relic, so we can send signals to all three at the same time. For each integration, we figured out how to set up the exporters, enter the necessary credentials, and make sure the telemetry showed up in the relevant UIs.

Chapter 9: Visualizing and Alerting Telemetry Data

Overview

In this chapter, our focus will be on transforming all the telemetry data we collect into useful insights through visualization and alerting. We'll learn how to connect Grafana to our OpenTelemetry backends, build dashboards that show key service metrics and logs for real-time awareness and historical analysis. We'll route traces to Jaeger and take a look at the UI to see how distributed spans, dependencies, and end-to-end performance work together. We're going to use Prometheus as our time series engine to create PromQL queries. These queries will help us spot usage patterns, error spikes, and latency trends.

After this, we'll set these dashboards up by defining and tuning alert rules in both Prometheus and Grafana. That way, we'll get an immediate notification of any issues that pop up. As we move through each step, we'll be building and sharing visualizations and simulating operational events. This will make sure our system alerts us quickly and enables us to respond quickly.

Building Dashboards in Grafana

We keep periodically collect a wealth of signals, metrics from Prometheus, logs from Loki, and traces from Tempo, but without effective visualization, this data is just noise. When something goes wrong or a spike appears, we want instant insight into what is happening, where, and why. And that's where the Graphana comes in. The ability to build and share dynamic dashboards in Grafana makes the difference between flying blind and catching issues before they become incidents.

In this recipe, we will learn to connect Grafana to our OTel-powered backends and then build dashboards that surface the most important signals in a way our teams can use and share.

Connecting Grafana to OTel Backends

We will begin by hooking Grafana up to our OTel data sources:

Add Prometheus as a Data Source

- Open Grafana and go to **Settings > Data Sources**. And then, choose **Prometheus**, and set the URL to the Prometheus server (for example, **`http://prometheus-server.observability.svc.cluster.local:9090`**).
- Finally, click the **Save & Test** such that the Grafana will show if the connection works.

Add Loki for Logs

- For this, go to the Data Sources, and then select **Loki**.
- Next, you then enter the Loki endpoint URL, and save and test the connection.

With this, the Grafana is ready to query all the metrics, logs, and traces flowing through our OpenTelemetry pipelines.

Building and Sharing a Dashboard

Create New Dashboard

Here, at first, click **+** on the left sidebar, then **Dashboard**. After this, add a new panel.

Then, for metrics, select the Prometheus data source, and type a query such as:

```
node_cpu_seconds_total
```

Here, you adjust filters or you may simply group by labels (for example, by node, instance, or job) to tailor the panel to our use case.

And, for logs, we just add another panel, then select Loki, and we enter a query such as:

```
{job="order-api"} |~ "error|warning"
```

This quickly shows real-time error or warning logs for a specific app or service.

Customize Visualization

Here, we can choose between time series, bar graphs, tables, or heatmaps, depending on the data. After this, we can set the thresholds, value mappings, or custom units to highlight what matters.

Save and Share

And then, we just must click **Save Dashboard**, give it a meaningful name, share it with teammates by copying the link, or set permissions for the organization.

By connecting Grafana to our OTel data sources and designing actionable dashboards, we empower ourselves to spot issues, monitor health, and keep everyone in the loop, all with real-time visual feedback that is easy to use and share. This is where all our telemetry finally comes together, turning raw signals into insight.

Visualizing Traces in Jaeger

When a request passes through several microservices or components, issues can be hard to diagnose without end-to-end visibility. Here, we want to understand not just when something fails, but precisely where time is spent, which service is slow, and how dependencies interact. And, the Jaeger gives us this distributed tracing insight. So here, the challenge is to ensure traces from our OpenTelemetry pipeline reach Jaeger, and that we can analyze them interactively in the UI.

Routing Traces to Jaeger

To begin with, we will first make sure the Collector is configured to export traces to Jaeger:

```
exporters:
  jaeger:
    endpoint: "jaeger-
collector.observability.svc.cluster.local:14250"
    tls:
      insecure: true
```

Next, we then wire the Jaeger exporter into the traces pipeline:

```
service:
  pipelines:
    traces:
      receivers: [otlp, jaeger, zipkin]
      processors: [batch]
      exporters: [jaeger]
```

After applying this configuration and restarting the Collector, every trace that enters the Collector will be forwarded to Jaeger.

Generating and Sending Traces

Here, we will need to trigger some requests in the instrumented applications, or we must use a sample client that emits OpenTelemetry traces. These traces will now flow into Jaeger through the Collector.

So, to do this:

- Navigate to the Jaeger web interface, usually at **`http://<jaeger-host>:16686`**.
- In the left sidebar, select the service name from the dropdown. And, set time filters or search for a specific operation (for example, **`/api/order`**).
- Click **Find Traces** to see recent traces. And, then click on a trace to open the detailed view. The UI displays a waterfall of spans, showing which components participated, the timing for each span, and where errors or latency occurred.
- Expand spans to see attributes, tags, logs, and parent-child relationships.

We can also use the Jaeger's dependency graph to visualize how the services connect and communicate.

Validating Trace Flow

As you generate more requests, watch traces appear live. If traces are missing, check Collector logs for exporter errors or misconfigurations. If you see data, confirm that span attributes (such as HTTP methods, user IDs, or custom tags) are visible and correct.

Querying Prometheus for Service Patterns

We might have thousands of metrics flowing into Prometheus, CPU usage, request rates, error counts, latency percentiles, but unless we know how to query and visualize these, we are left guessing when incidents strike or usage changes. Being able to write precise PromQL queries and interpret time series graphs is what turns data into actionable service patterns. So, in this recipe, we will learn to connect to Prometheus, run the right queries, and graph our findings to answer real-world operational questions.

Open Grafana Explore Panel

In Grafana, click **Explore** and select the Prometheus data source.

Alternatively, we can open the Prometheus web UI, typically available at **`http://<prometheus-server>:9090`**.

Construct Query

Suppose we want to analyze HTTP request volume for a service. So here, we will start with a basic PromQL query:

```
sum(rate(http_requests_total{job="order-api"}[5m]))
```

Here, in the above query:

- **`http_requests_total`** is the metric tracking requests.
- **`job="order-api"`** filters for our specific service.
- **`rate(...[5m])`** calculates per-second rate over the last five minutes.
- **`sum(...)`** aggregates across all instances of the service.

We simply paste this into the query bar and execute.

Graph Results

In Grafana, the results appear as a time series graph, showing how request rates change over time. And, in the Prometheus UI, we can just click **Execute** and then **Graph** to see the curve.

We can also try to tweak the query to group by HTTP method or status code:

```
sum by (method, status) (rate(http_requests_total{job="order-api"}[5m]))
```

This helps us spot which types of requests are most frequent or causing issues.

Now, to check error rates:

```
sum(rate(http_requests_total{job="order-api",
status=~"5.."}[5m]))
```

This surfaces only 5xx errors, indicating server issues.

Interpret Patterns

We can add more queries, like average or p95 latency:

```
histogram_quantile(0.95,
sum(rate(http_request_duration_seconds_bucket{job="order-api"}[5m])) by (le))
```

Or, if the resource consumption:

```
avg(node_cpu_seconds_total{instance=~"app.*"}) by (instance)
```

The more we write, run, and graph these queries, the better we'll understand usage patterns, plan for scaling, and respond quickly when something abnormal appears. These dashboards let us put all these patterns side-by-side, so the whole team can spot trends and outliers.

Creating Alert Rules in Grafana and Prometheus

While metrics and dashboards are key for observability, if we don't have well-crafted alerting, our response to outages or anomalies can be slow and reactive. The challenge is in setting up the right rules, spotting problems early without causing alert fatigue, and setting up notifications for the right teams. With Prometheus as our backend and Grafana as our visualization layer, we can create both backend and frontend alerts that watch for key thresholds, then trigger emails, Slack messages, or other actions automatically.

In the following, we will walk through each step, reasoning out the choices, and validating as we go:

Defining Alerts in Prometheus

In Prometheus, the alert rules are defined in YAML and loaded by the Prometheus server.

Suppose we want to alert when our "order-api" returns too many 5xx errors. We write a rule in a file called **alert.rules.yml**:

```
groups:
  - name: order-api-alerts
    rules:
      - alert: High5xxErrorRate
        expr: sum(rate(http_requests_total{job="order-api",
status=~"5.."}[5m])) > 5
        for: 2m
        labels:
          severity: critical
        annotations:
          summary: "High rate of 5xx errors detected on order-
api"
          description: "More than 5 errors/sec for 2 minutes"
```

In the above,

- The **expr** calculates the rate of 5xx responses over the last five minutes.
- The **for** field ensures the condition is sustained for at least two minutes before firing.

We then reload Prometheus to activate the new rule:

```
promtool check rules alert.rules.yml
# If no errors, then:
kubectl apply -f alert.rules.yml
```

Defining Alerts in Grafana

The Grafana allows us to set alert rules visually, right on dashboard panels. And, for this:

- We open a dashboard and click on a panel showing the target metric.
- We then click the **Alert** tab, then **Create Alert** (or **Edit Alert** in new Grafana versions).
- And, then we define a condition, for example:

WHEN: max() `of query A (your error rate metric)` **IS ABOVE 5** `for` **2m**

We then save the alert rule. And after this, the Grafana will now continuously evaluates this rule.

Simulating Alert

Let us see the alerting in action by simulating high error traffic.

In the app, generate requests that trigger 5xx errors, for example, by hitting an invalid endpoint or shutting down a dependency. We then need to watch the Grafana panel or Prometheus Alertmanager UI. After two minutes of sustained errors, the alert should fire.

When the error condition clears (errors drop below threshold), Grafana and Prometheus automatically resolve the alert, and you should receive a "resolved" notification.

By setting up practical alerting in both Prometheus and Grafana, and simulating real conditions, we make sure our observability system is not just passive monitoring, but an active, responsive tool for protecting our services. This closes the loop between detection and action, empowering us to maintain uptime and confidence as our environments scale.

Summary

During this chapter, we built practical skills in transforming raw telemetry into real-time operational insight through visualization and alerting. We began by connecting Grafana to our OpenTelemetry backends, then created dashboards that brought metrics and logs to life for the team, supporting live monitoring and sharing. We routed traces to Jaeger and practiced using its UI to analyze end-to-end transactions, spot latency, and explore dependencies across distributed systems.

Next, we learned to use PromQL to extract patterns and trends from our time series data, visualizing service usage, error rates, and latency over time. We saw how carefully crafted queries, combined with flexible visualizations, could answer tough operational questions and support data-driven decisions. Finally, we put these visualizations to work by setting up alert rules in both Prometheus and Grafana. We defined actionable thresholds, created notifications, and simulated incident scenarios, ensuring our observability setup is always ready to catch and escalate issues in real time. Every recipe combined hands-on steps, configuration, and validation, ensuring our monitoring was not just passive but truly actionable, closing the loop from signal collection to alert-driven response.

Index

A

B

C

D

E

F

G

H

I

J

K

L

M

N

O

Epilogue

When you think about how quickly AI observability and security monitoring have gone from being new and exciting to being essential, it's pretty amazing. According to industry surveys, the adoption of AI monitoring jumped from 42% of organizations in 2024 to 54% in 2025. We've reached a point where it's not just a good idea, it's a necessity to keep a close eye on our AI. And this is only the beginning. By 2028, about a third of all enterprise software applications will include AI agents that can work on their own. With so many AI-driven decisions on the horizon, it's going to be crucial to have robust oversight. It's no surprise that the market for AI observability tools is expected to skyrocket past $10 billion by 2033. We can't unleash a bunch of agentic AI systems without having safety measures like observability and security monitoring in place.

So, what might those safety rails look like in the future? For one, observability itself will become smarter and more automated. We may even have AI systems monitoring other AI systems. In the future, models might flag their own performance declines and suggest retraining, and data pipelines might automatically switch to backup sources when anomalies arise. This kind of self-monitoring, when paired with human oversight, can catch problems early on before they get out of hand.

As far as security goes, AI is going to be an increasingly important ally. Those machine learning models can sift through network traffic and user behavior at speeds that are impossible for humans to match. They can spot threats that might otherwise go unnoticed. AI tools already help security teams find and block bad devices and activity as it happens. Since attackers are probably using AI too, having smart security monitoring is probably our best defense. In fact, 46% of tech leaders say that better observability has reduced security risks in their business. The combination of observability and security means that future systems will be able to detect faults in themselves and fend off external threats more effectively.

Most importantly, these practices won't just be for IT departments. They'll be used in every area that uses AI. When it comes to healthcare, we've got to keep a close eye on diagnostic AI to make sure it's safe and accurate. In finance, we've got to keep a close eye on algorithms managing investments or loans to avoid hidden bias or errors. In transportation, observability is key to keeping autonomous vehicles safe. Without it, a self-driving car might not realize something important is wrong with a sensor. In all these cases, AI observability and security monitoring are like a safety net, making sure that as we trust more in machines, we can quickly catch and fix any problems. We're also seeing more and more pressure for transparency and accountability. The people in charge are starting to say that AI systems have to be able to explain what they're doing and be able to be checked. So, what we've talked about, like transparency and logging, is going to become not just good practices but legal requirements in a lot of industries.

At the end of the day, trust is what it all comes down to. For people to start using AI in their daily lives, they need to know it's working properly and they can control it. AI observability is key to building that trust. When an AI can explain its decisions and we can keep an eye on how it's behaving, it becomes way less of a black box. And if we pair that with strong security monitoring to guard against tampering, we've got the foundation for truly reliable, trustworthy AI. When we make sure that AI is both observable and secure, we can be sure that it'll stay our tool and not the other way around.

Despite this, I'm still hopeful that the creativity behind AI's growth is now being used to keep it in check. I started this book with a midnight wake-up, which taught me a big lesson about why we can't ever leave our ideas on the table. In the future, I think we'll see a trend where every AI has its own dashboard and watchdog, and organizations encourage a "trust but verify" approach for all intelligent systems.

Thank You

www.ingramcontent.com/pod-product-compliance
Lightning Source LLC
Chambersburg PA
CBHW080216170726
48282CB00030B/1139
9789349174399